The Book of
Ruth

This Guide has been divided into two parts. The first part relates to a historical prospective. The second part relates to prophecy.

Common People Series

THE PURPOSE OF THIS GUIDE

Mark 12:37...And the common people heard him gladly

The twelfth chapter of Mark begins with Jesus teaching a parable and as usual, the Pharisees, Sadducees and scribes began to flaunt their scholarly knowledge and tried to snare Him in His own words. In the background, is another group of people. They were the common people.... ***And the common people heard him gladly.***

As in Biblical times, common people are not less intelligent but many do lack confidence and encouragement to read the Word of God. The lack of confidence in our ability to read and learn the scriptures discourages us from actually reading them. What seems as a lack of confidence in ourselves, however, is wrongly placed false humility. It is our lack of FAITH in the Holy Spirit to teach us to skillfully handle the Word of God.

This book includes general Bible knowledge and deeper studies. But it's intent is not just to impart knowledge. Ultimately, it is to help you increase your faith in the Holy Spirit that He **will** guide and teach **you** to skillfully handle the Word of God. You may at first follow this guide to the letter. But it won't be long before you are allowing the Holy Spirit to lead you through your own reading.
John 16:13 Howbeit when he, the Spirit of truth, is come, he will guide you into all truth: for he shall not speak of himself; but whatsoever he shall hear, that shall he speak.

The Bible is the inspired Word of God and consists of 66 books. You can follow this inspiration from one book of the Bible to the next by looking for shadows, patterns, similiarities and cross references. I have included my own studies to help you learn how to recognize some of these.

This guide will also be of great value to those who are searching the scriptures for the deeper things of God. ***1 Corinthians 2:10 But God hath revealed them unto us by his Spirit: for the Spirit searcheth all things, yea, the deep things of God.*** The format enables you to visualize small details that our brains may choose to skip because of information overload. It is invaluable in discerning the proper context of each passage while organizing people, places, dates and sequence of events.

HOW TO USE THIS GUIDE

1. **You must use the King James Bible.** All answers correspond to the King James Bible. There is no substitute.

2. The chapters are divided into sections. Each section has two pages. The lower page (NOTES) is for you to fill in the blanks and record your own notes. I have intentionally used generic pictures that are black and white, faceless, and unremarkable to avoid preconceived notions and ideas.

3. The opposite page (GUIDE) is a duplicate and has the completed answers written in *script*. Also written in *script* are my notes. Some of these notes are as simple as definitions of words or that may be unfamiliar and possibly hinder the understanding. Others are deep Bible studies that leaves us in awe of God's Word.

4. <u>This is very important</u>. Answer each question in numerical order because they are numbered according to the sequence of events. Some pages contain a lot of information and are very busy. Each question already has the first letter completed.   ① ② ③

5. The only type questions are complete the verses from your reading that are fresh on your mind. There is not multiple choice, True/False, matching and etc. which tend to distract you from your train of thoughts.

6. <u>Don't try to study outside sources to clarify the meaning.</u> <u>There is no historical or archaeological information from antiquities or Greek/Hebrew lexicons included</u>. This is not necessary because the King James Bible is plenary meaning complete. If you want to do a deeper study, search the Bible for similiar verses, phrases or ideas. These can be easily found by using a concordance (a book that lists words of the Bible in alphabetical order). The Webster's 1828 Dictionary is an excellent source to find definitions to biblical words that may have dropped out of today's vocabulary.

7. Maps are used for general locations only. They are not exactly to scale but serve to keep places and events in context.

THE BOOK OF RUTH

Background

The only background we need is provided for us throughout the Bible. We don't need archaelogical evidence, antiquities or whatever. Trust the Bible to be complete in itself. To help gain confidence in the Bible, try to find these facts as your are reading through it.

The Book of Ruth takes place during the time of the judges in Israel. At this time the Israelites were doing what was right in their own eyes which was evil in the sight of the Lord. When famine came, a man named Elimelech left Bethlehem, the Promised Land, and took his wife and two sons to Moab. Moab was a godless country that had previously refused to give the Israelites bread when they were in the wilderness after leaving Egypt. Elimelech and his two sons died, leaving Naomi with two Moabite daughter-in-laws, Orpah and Ruth.

Ruth returns to Bethlehem with Naomi but Orpah stays in Moab. After returning in what seems like a hopeless situation for the two widows, through God's providence, Ruth marries a wealthy man who loves her dearly. The couple have a son, whom Naomi will raise up in her dead husband's name according to the laws of Israel. His name is Obed and is in the royal lineage of King David and the Lord Jesus Christ.

The Book of Ruth is only 4 chapters but is rich in symbolisms of the Jewish feasts, salvation and prophecies of the end times.

...and the common people heard him gladly. Mark 12:37

Read Chapter 1

Psalm 119:103 How sweet are thy words unto my taste! yea, sweeter than honey to my mouth!

God works by miracle and providence. Providence is when God directs natural occurences for a specific outcome. When you follow God and do what is right, God will lead you through His providence.

God had chosen a certain man for a certain purpose.

V.1 Now it came to pass in the days when the *judges* ruled, that there was a *famine* in the land. And a *certain* man of ———— *to dwell temporarily* *Bethlehemjudah* went to *sojourn* in the country of *Moab*, he, and his wife, and his two sons.

The country of Moab resulted from the incest of Lot and one of his daughters after the destruction of Sodom and Gomorrah.

Mediterranean Sea

Dor

Taanach

Sochoh

Jordan River

Gibeon

Jerusalem

Bethlehem

Gath

Judah

Dead Sea

Moab

Ammon

Genesis 19:35 And they made their father drink wine that night also: and the younger arose, and lay with him; and he perceived not when she lay down, nor when she arose.
Genesis 19:36 <u>Thus were both the daughters of Lot with child by their father.</u>
<u>Genesis 19:37 And the first born bare a son, and called his name Moab: the same is the father of the Moabites unto this day.</u>
Genesis 19:38 And the younger, she also bare a son, and called his name Benammi:<u> the same is the father of the children of Ammon unto this day</u>.

Moabites refused to give bread to the children of Israel in the wilderness. Now there is a famine and Elimelech takes his family there for food?

Deuteronomy 23:3 An <u>Ammonite or Moabite shall not enter into the congregation of the LORD; even to their tenth generation</u> shall they not enter into the congregation of the LORD for ever:
Deuteronomy 23:4 <u>Because they met you not with bread and with water in the way, when ye came forth out of Egypt; and because they hired against thee Balaam the son of Beor of Pethor of Mesopotamia, to curse thee</u>.

V.1 Now it came to pass in the days when the j_____ ruled, that there was a f_____ in the land. And a c_____ man of B_____ went to s_____ in the country of M_____, he, and his wife, and his two sons.

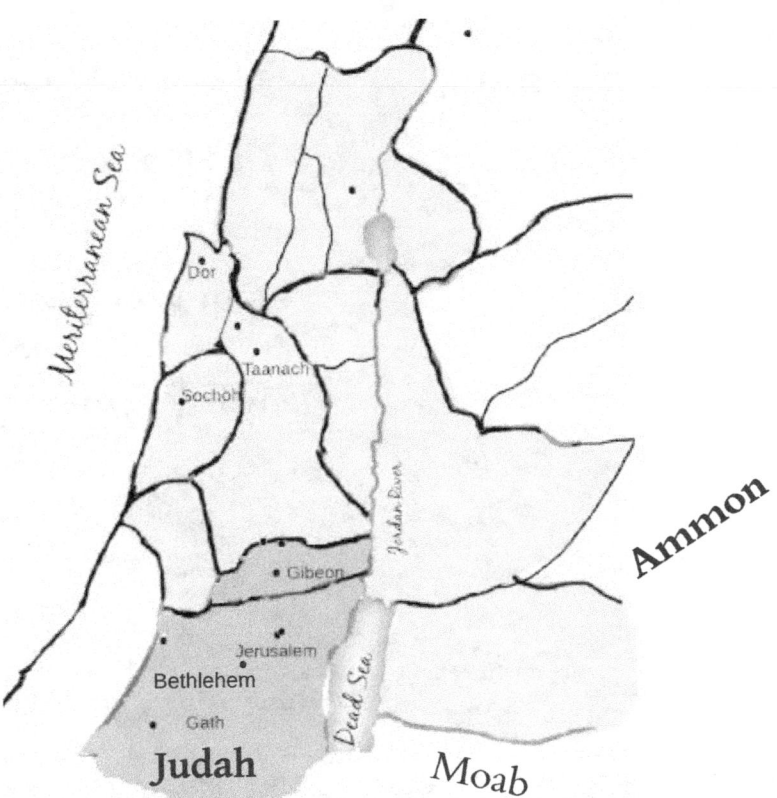

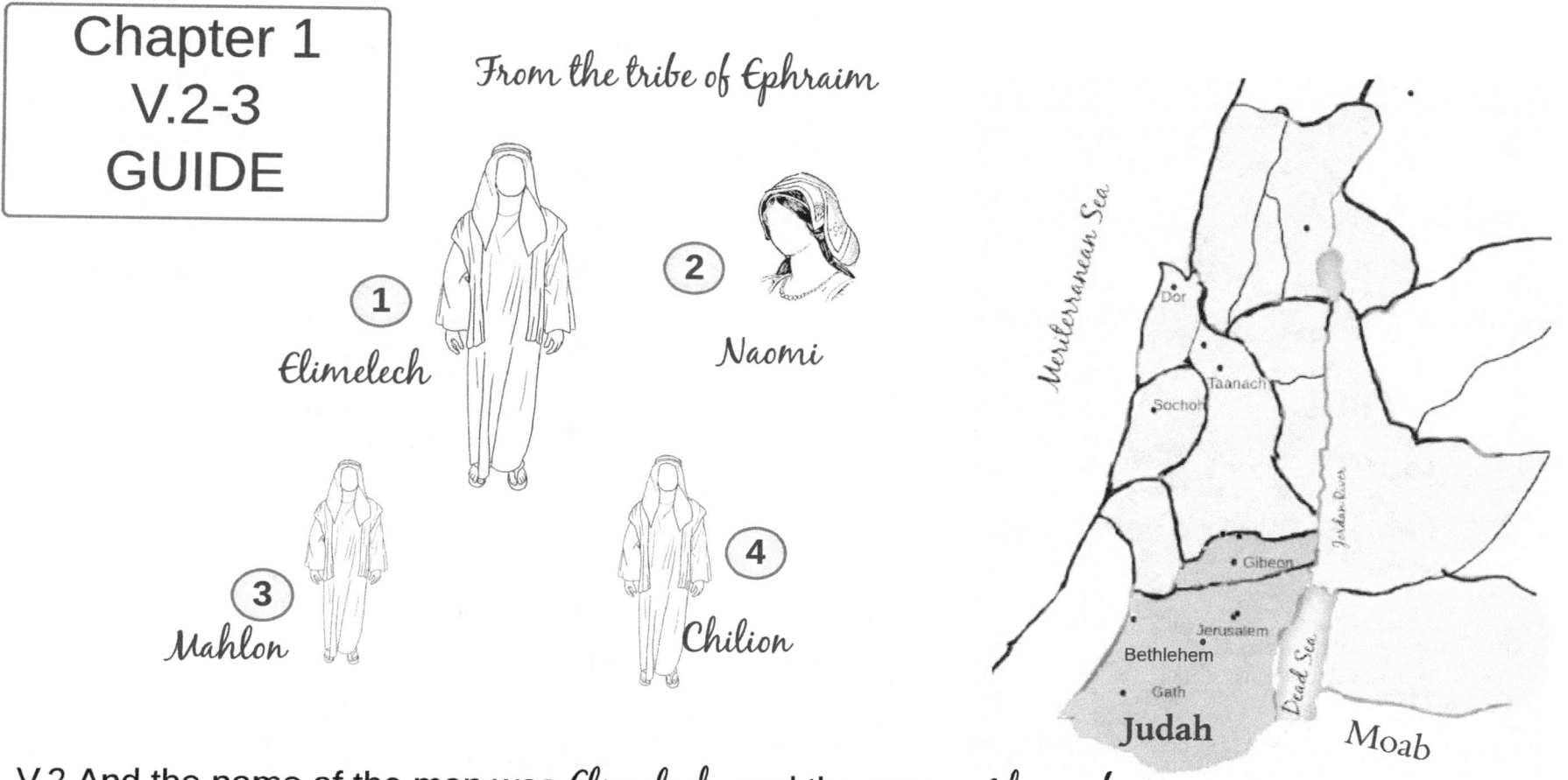

From the tribe of Ephraim

1 Elimelech

2 Naomi

3 Mahlon

4 Chilion

V.2 And the name of the man was Elimelech, and the name of his wife Naomi, and the name of his two sons Mahlon and Chilion, Ephrathites of Bethlehemjudah. And they came into the country of Moab, and continued there.

only went to sojourn for a while but stayed

V.3 And Elimelech Naomi's husband died; and she was left, and her two sons.

Elimelech

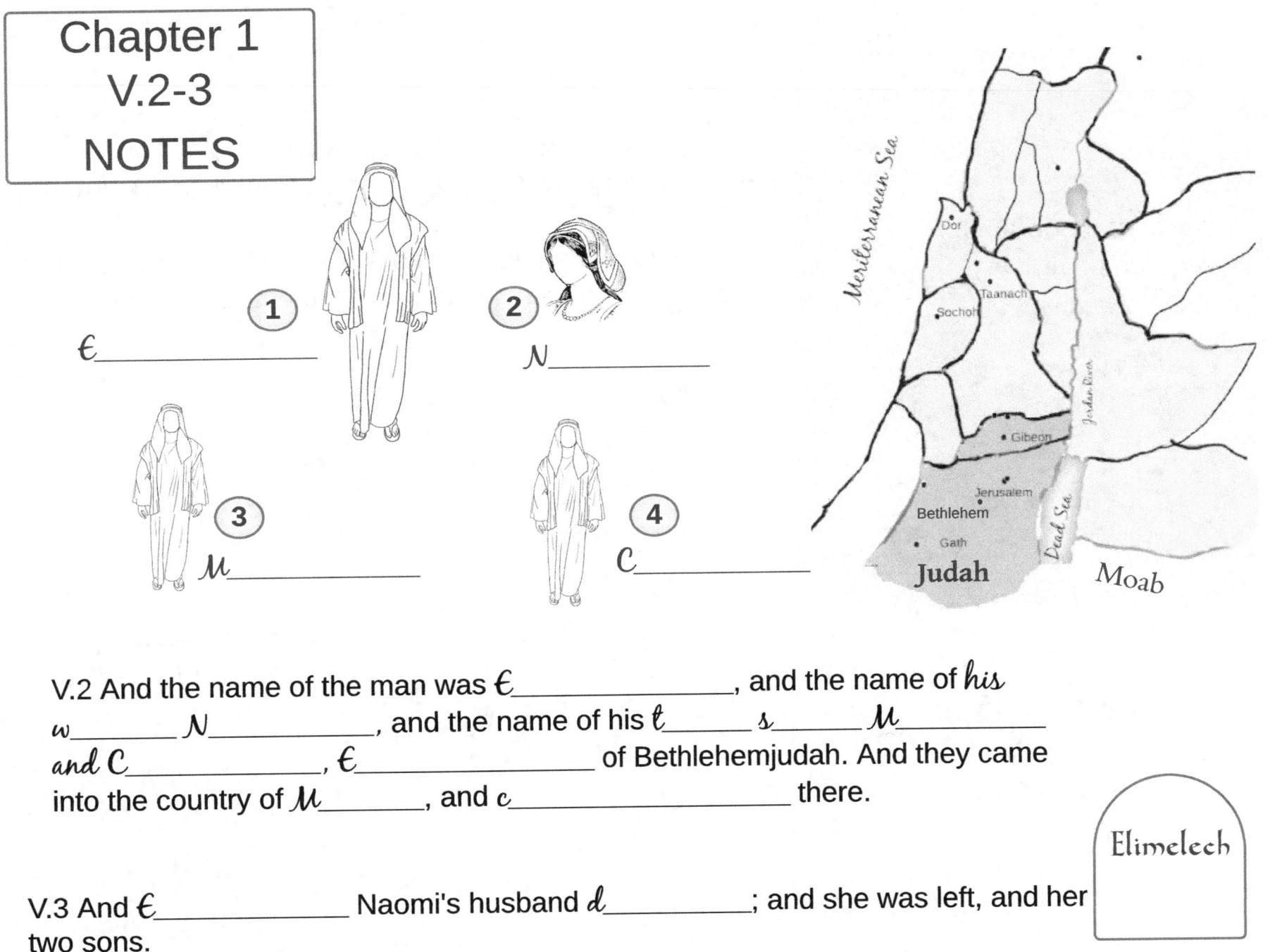

Chapter 1 V.2-3 NOTES

1. E_____

2. N_____

3. M_____

4. C_____

Judah

Moab

Elimelech

V.2 And the name of the man was E_____, and the name of *his* w_____ N_____, and the name of his l_____ s_____ M_____ and C_____, E_____ of Bethlehemjudah. And they came into the country of M_____, and c_____ there.

V.3 And E_____ Naomi's husband d_____; and she was left, and her two sons.

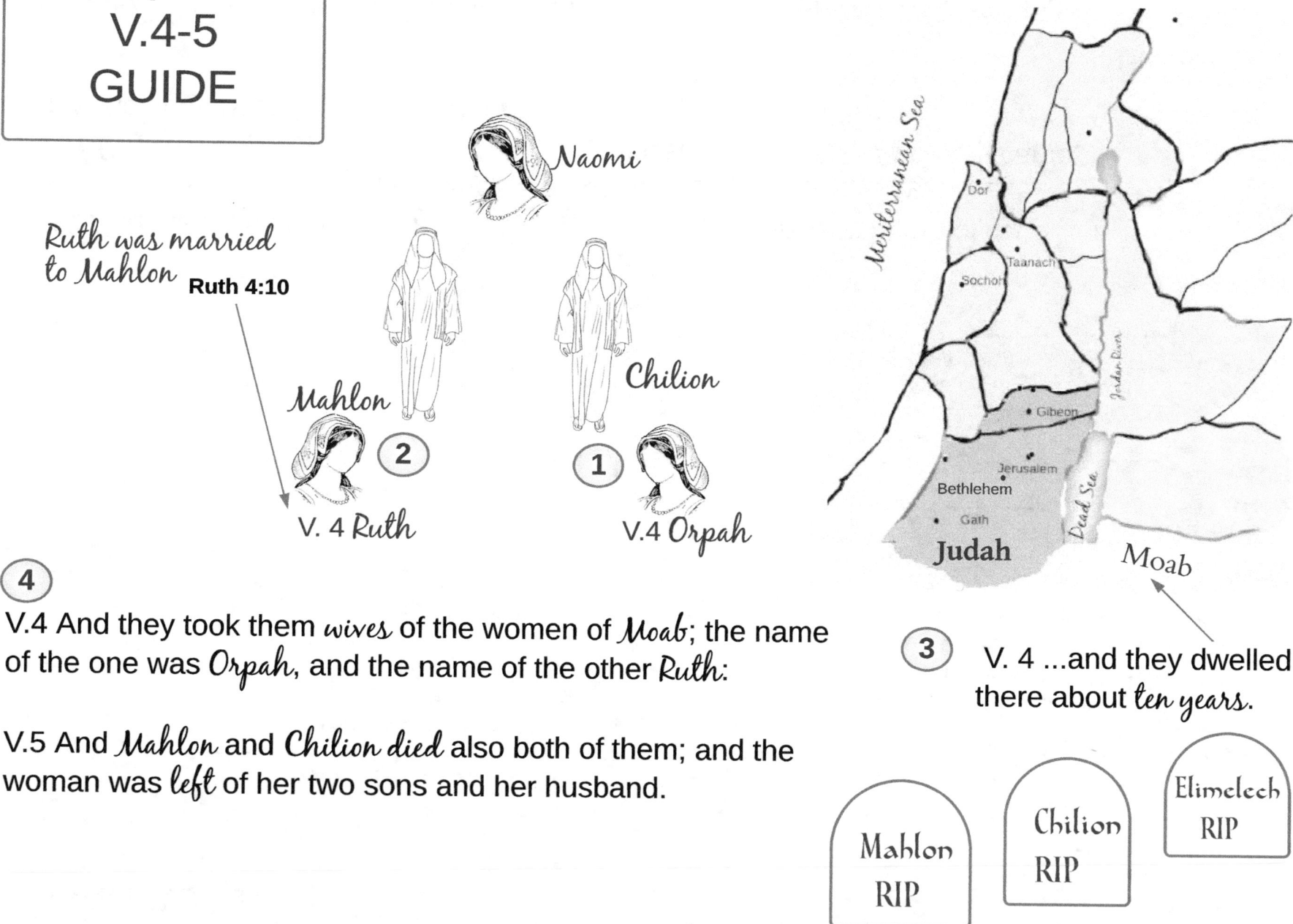

Ruth was married
to Mahlon **Ruth 4:10**

Naomi

Mahlon

Chilion

2

1

V. 4 Ruth

V.4 Orpah

4

V.4 And they took them *wives* of the women of *Moab*; the name
of the one was *Orpah*, and the name of the other *Ruth*:

V.5 And *Mahlon* and *Chilion died* also both of them; and the
woman was *left* of her two sons and her husband.

3 V. 4 ...and they dwelled
there about *ten years*.

Mahlon
RIP

Chilion
RIP

Elimelech
RIP

Judah *Moab*

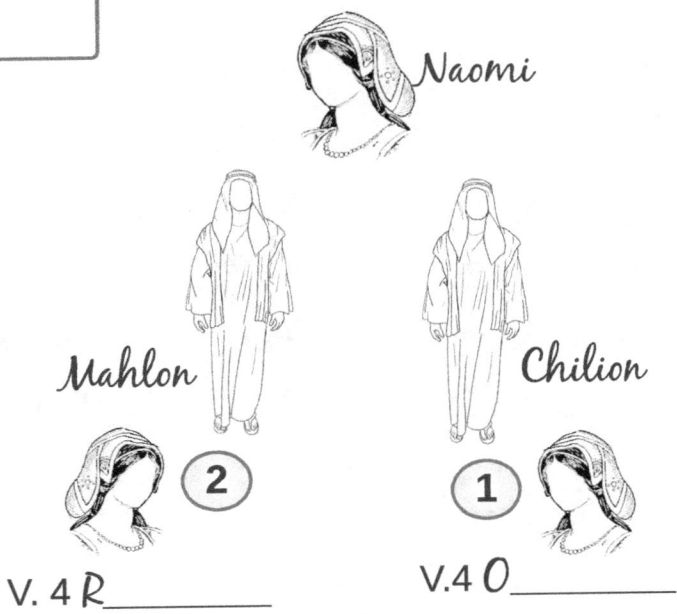

Naomi

Mahlon

Chilion

② ①

V. 4 R_____   V.4 O_____

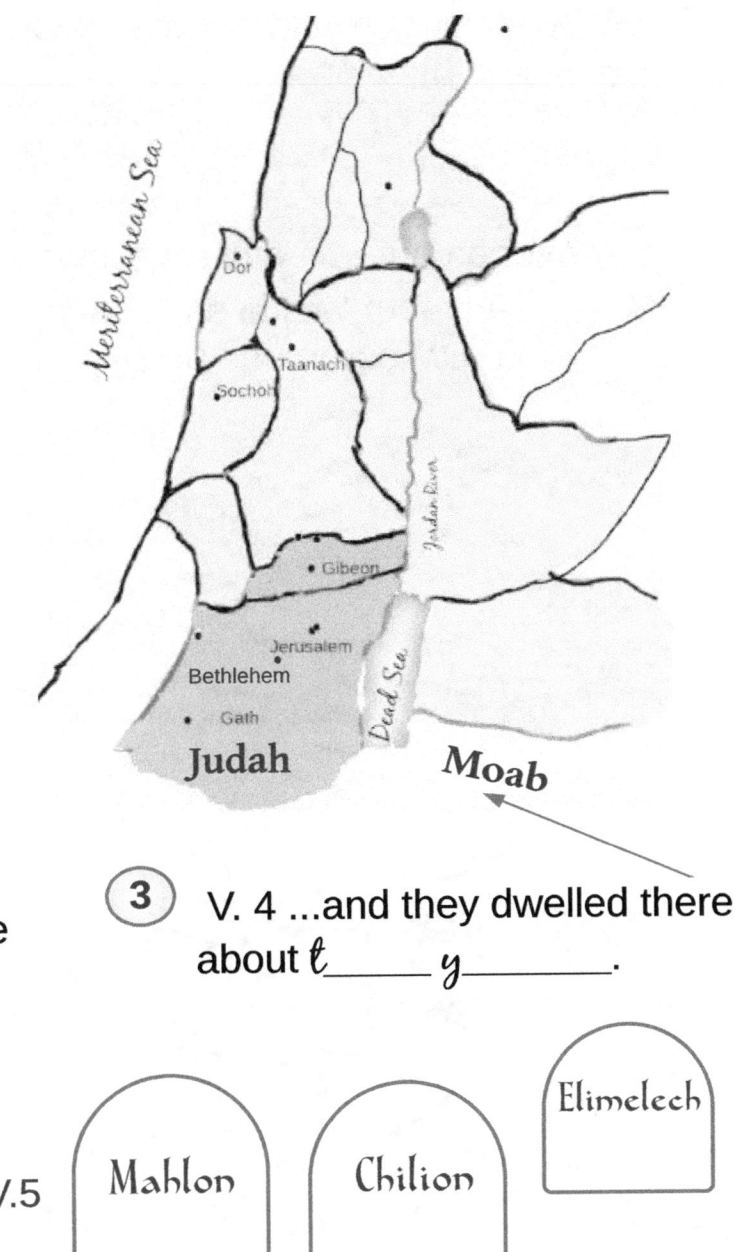

Judah   Moab

V.4 And they took them w_____ of the women of
M_____; the name of the one was O_____, and the
name of the other R_____:
V.5 And M_____ and C_____ d_____ also
both of them; and the woman was l_____ of her two sons
and her husband.

③ V. 4 ...and they dwelled there
about t_____ y_____.

④ V.5

Mahlon   Chilion   Elimelech

Ruth does not know how God has been working in her life. "Giving them bread" means the barley is growing which is used to make bread. She will meet her future husband because of this crop.

When Jesus was born, The Lord also visited Bethlehem. Only this time, He gave them the Bread of Life.

John 6:35, Luke 1:68

2 V.6 ...for she had heard in the country of Moab how that the LORD had visited his people in giving them bread.

Mediterranean Sea

Dor

Taanach

Sochoh

Gibeon

Jordan River

Jerusalem

Bethlehem

Gath

Judah

Dead Sea

Moab

V. 10 Surely we will return with thee unto thy people.

Orpah wanted to go but she did not have the conviction of Ruth.

Orpah

Ruth

Naomi

1 V.6 Then she arose with her daughters in law, that she might return from the country of Moab

3 V.8...the LORD deal kindly with you, as ye have dealt with the dead, and with me.

V.9 The LORD grant you that ye may find rest, each of you in the house of her husband.

Ruth does not know but she will rest in the house of her husband because of her trust in God..

Mediterranean Sea

Dor

Taanach

Sochoh

Gibeon

Jerusalem

Bethlehem

Gath

Judah

Jordan River

Dead Sea

Moab

2

V.6 ...for she had heard in the country of Moab how that the LORD had v_____ his people in g_____ them b_____.

V. 10 S_____ we will return with thee unto t_____ p_____.

Orpah

Ruth

Naomi

1

V.6 Then she arose with her daughters in law, that she might r_____ from the country of M_____.

3 V.8...the LORD deal kindly with you, as ye have d_____ with the d_____, and with m_____.
V.9 The LORD grant you that ye m_____ f_____ r_____, each of you in the h_____ of her h_____.

Ruth

Orpah

Naomi

V.11..Turn again, my daughters: why will ye go with me? *are there yet any more sons in my wombs, that they may be your husbands?*

V.12 Turn again, my daughters, go your way; for *I am too old* to have an husband. If I should say, I have *hope, if I should* have an husband also to night, and should also bear sons;

V. 13 *Would ye tarry for them till they were grown?* would ye stay for them from having husbands? nay, my daughters; for it grieveth me much for your sakes that *the hand of the LORD is gone out against me.*

Romans 8:28 And we know that all things work together for good to them that love God, to them who are the called according to his purpose.

Because of her age she lost hope that she would ever have a son again. Under Israelite law, that son would marry Orpah or Ruth to keep her husband's name from being put out.

Deuteronomy 25:5 If brethren dwell together, and one of them die, and have no child, the wife of the dead shall not marry <u>without unto a stranger: her husband's brother shall go in unto her, and take her to him to wife, and perform the duty of an husband's brother unto her.</u>

What she did not know were the plans that God had for her. Jer.29:11

Naomi doesn't know what God'a purpose is for her. All things will work out for good for her.

Ruth

Orpah

Naomi

V.11..Turn again, my daughters: why will ye go with me? are there yet any more s_____ in my w_____, that they may be y_____ h_____?

V.12 Turn again, my daughters, go your way; for I am t_____o_____ to have an husband. If I should say, I have hope, i____ I s_____ have an husband also to night, and should also bear sons;

V. 13 Would ye t_____ for them t_____ they were g_____? would ye stay for them from having husbands? nay, my daughters; for it grieveth me much for your sakes that the h_____ of the L_____ is g_____ out a_____ m_____.

Instead of following a widowed woman who could never provide for her into a land where she may not be accepted and treated well, Orpah did what seemed sensible and went back to her people and her gods.

V.14 And *they* lifted up their voice, and *wept again*: and Orpah *kissed her mother in law*; but Ruth clave unto her.
V.15 And she said, *Behold, thy sister in law is gone back unto her people*, and *unto her gods*: return thou after thy sister in law.

The Moabites worshipped a false god called Chemosh.

1Kings 11:7 Then did Solomon build an high place for <u>Chemosh, the abomination of Moab.</u> (*Moab was an abomination to God because of Chemosh*)

The Moabites believed in child sacrifice to Chemosh.
Later in history, the king of Moab sacrificed his eldest son to Chemosh when they lost in a battle to Israel.

2Kings 3:26 And when <u>the king of Moab</u> saw that the battle was too sore for him, he took with him seven hundred men that drew swords, to break through even unto the king of Edom: but they could not.
2Kings 3:27 <u>Then he took his eldest son that should have reigned in his stead, and offered him for a burnt offering upon the wall.</u> And there was great indignation against Israel: and they departed from him, and returned to their own land.

Mediterranean Sea

Dor
Taanach
Sochoh
Gibeon
Jerusalem
Bethlehem
Gath
Judah
Dead Sea
Jordan River
Moab

Orpah

Chapter 1
V.14-15
NOTES

V.14 And t_____ lifted up their voice, and w_____ a_____: and O_____ k_____ her mother in law; but Ruth clave unto her.

V.15 And she said, Behold, thy sister in law is g_____ b_____ u_____ her p_____, and unto her g_____: return thou after thy sister in law.

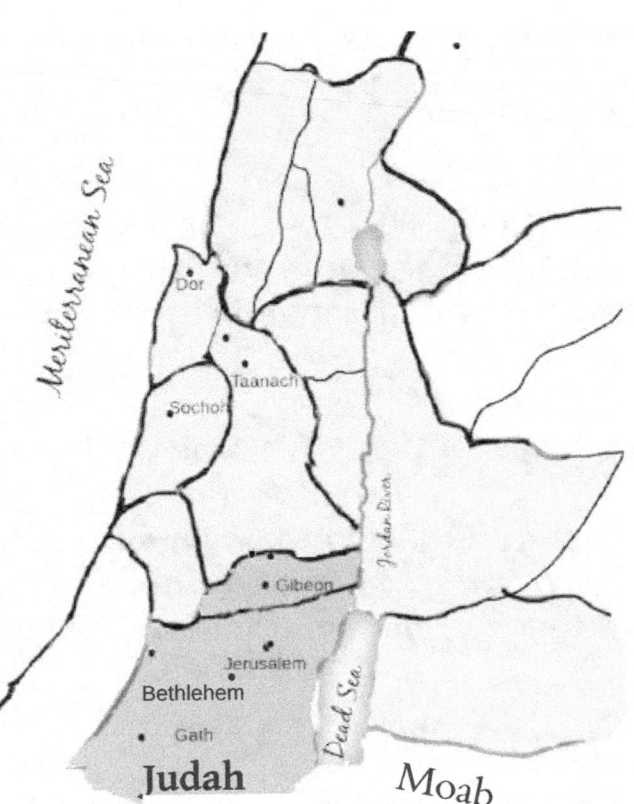

Orpah

 Ruth

V.16 for whither thou goest, I will go; and where thou lodgest, I will lodge: *thy people shall be my people, and thy God my God:*

V.17 Where thou diest, will I die, and there will I be buried: the LORD do so to me, and more also, if ought but *death part thee and me.*

Naomi was in the depths of despair. She felt as if she had lost everything; her husband, her only 2 sons, and even God had turned against her also. She could go back to Bethlehem with the only 2 people she had left that she dearly loved, Ruth and Orpah. However; since God had gone against her and as Moabite women and strangers to Israel, Naomi, did not think Bethlehem would be a good place for daughter-in-laws to start a new life. Thinking more of them, than of her own dire situation, she told them to depart from her and go back to their people and their own gods.

But at what seemed to be the lowest point in Naomi's life, Ruth refused to turn her back on her. She assured Naomi that she would never lose her except when they were to be separated by death. Ruth did not do what seemed sensible for her own welfare, but she reaffirmed her committment to her dead husband by following her living mother-in-law.

Ruth's decision depended upon her willingness to forsake all for Naomi, her people and what would become the most important of all, the God of Israel.

Ruth

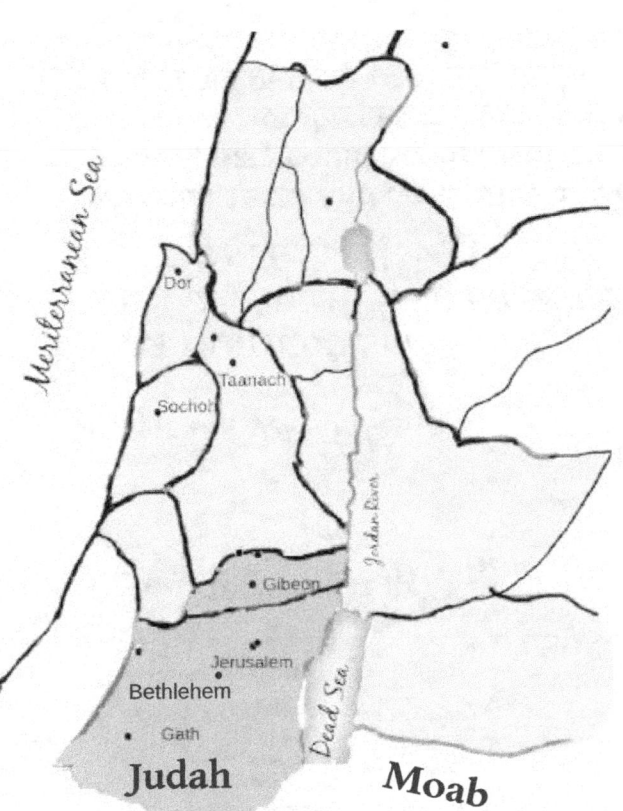

V.16 for whither thou goest, I will go; and where thou lodgest, I will lodge: t_____ p_____ shall be m____ p_____, and t_____ g_____ m___ g_____:

V.17 Where thou diest, will I die, and there will I be buried: the LORD do so to me, and more also, if ought but d_____ p_____ t_____ and m_____.

They speak as if they hardly recognized her because of her bitterness

Ruth

Naomi

1 V.19...that all the city was moved about them, and they said, *Is this Naomi?*

God had not dealt bitterly with her. He was usng her according to His purpose.

2 V.20 ... Call me *not Naomi*, call me *Mara*: for the Almighty hath dealt *very bitterly* with me.

Not true. Ruth will be better to her than 7 sons. Ruth 4:15

V.21 *I went out full* and the LORD hath brought me home *again empty*: why then call ye me Naomi, seeing the LORD hath *testified against me*, and the *Almighty hath afflicted me?*

Not true. The Lord will testify for her when the time comes.

Mara means very bitter

As the children of Israel was leaving Egypt, they came upon bitter waters called Marah.

Exodus 15:23 And when they came to Marah, they could not drink of the waters of Marah, for they were bitter: therefore the name of it was called Marah.

Mediterranean Sea

Dor

Taanach

Socho

Jordan River

Gibeon

Jerusalem

Bethlehem

Gath

Judah

Dead Sea

Moab

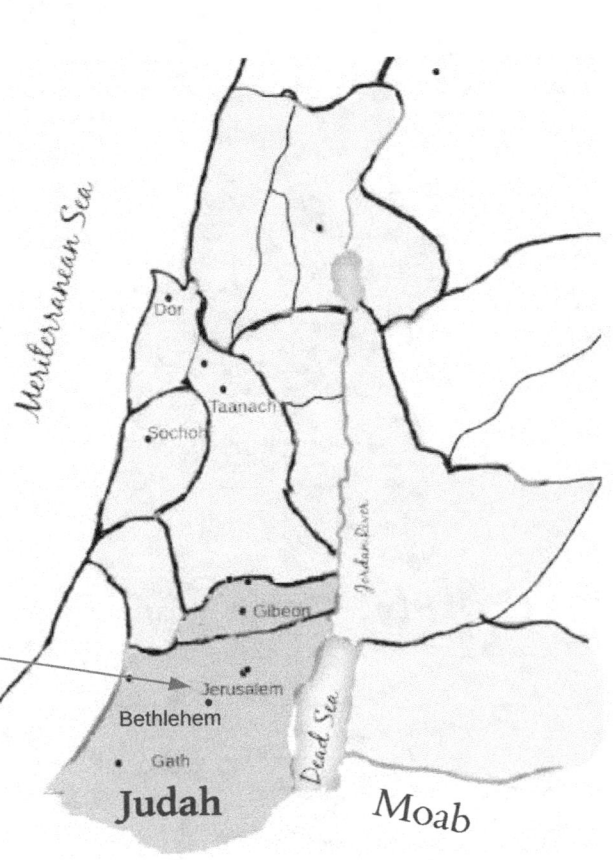

Ruth

Naomi

① V.19...that all the city
was moved about
them, and they said,
I____ t_____
N_____?

② V.20 ... Call me n_____
N_____, call me
M_____: for the Almighty
hath dealt v_____
b_____ with me.

V.21 I w_____ o_____ f_____
and the LORD hath brought me
home again empty: why then call
ye me Naomi, seeing the LORD
hath t_____
a_____ me, and the
A_____ hath
a_____ m_____?

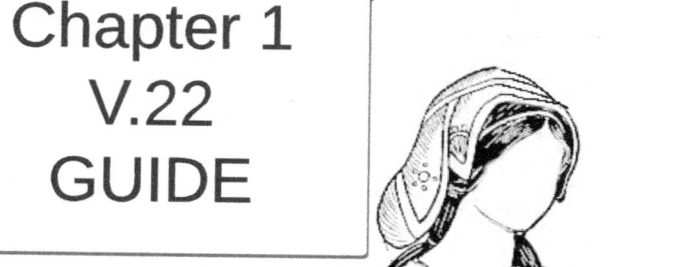

Naomi

Ruth

V.22 So Naomi returned, and Ruth the Moabitess, her daughter in law, with her, which returned out of the country of Moab: and they came to *Bethlehem* in the *beginning of barley harvest.*

By God's providence workers were needed in the fields.
God controlled the circumstances where Ruth would meet her future husband.

Mediterranean Sea

Dor

Taanach

Sochoh

Gibeon

Jordan River

Jerusalem

Bethlehem

Dead Sea

Gath

Judah

Moab

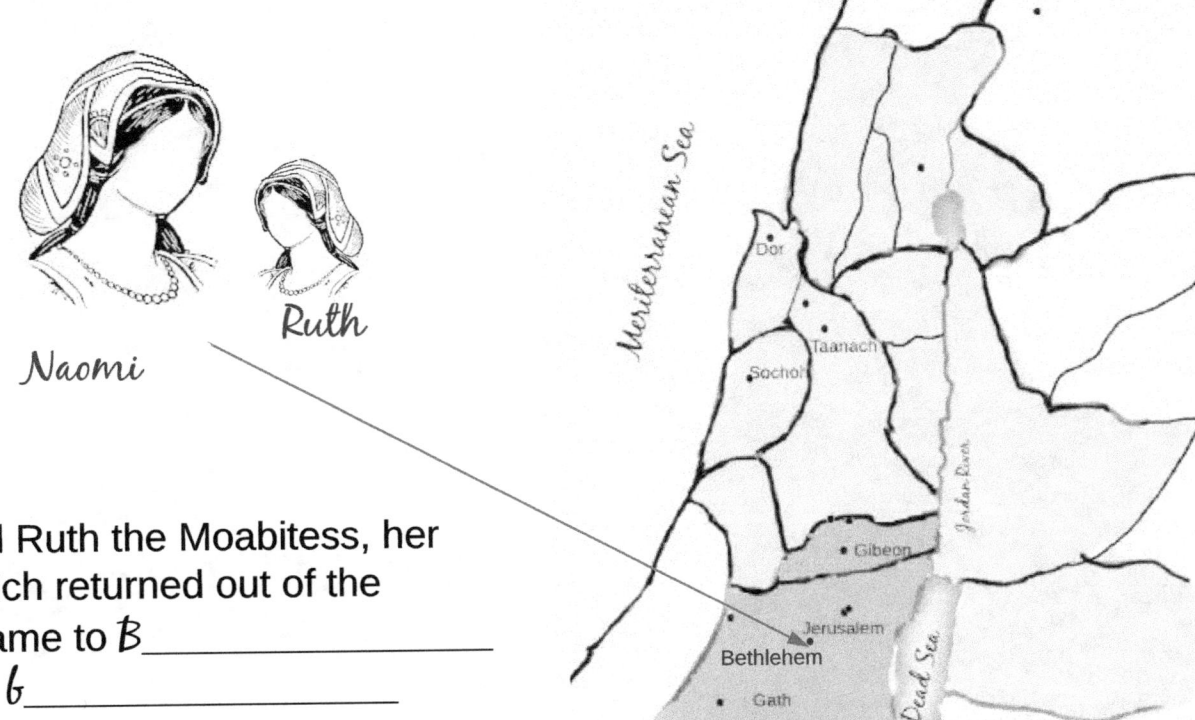

Naomi

Ruth

V.22 So Naomi returned, and Ruth the Moabitess, her daughter in law, with her, which returned out of the country of Moab: and they came to B_____ in the b_____ of b_____ h_____.

Read Chapter 2

John 6:63...the words that I speak unto you, they are spirit, and they are life.

① V.1 Naomi

kinsman-family relative.

V.2 Ruth the Moabitess

③

corn is a generic term for grain. The barley is a corn. It is not the same meaning as our corn crop today.

⑤ Go, my daughter.

Searching for grace.

② V.1 ...a kinsman of her husband's, a mighty man of wealth, of the family of Elimelech; and his name was Boaz.

④ V.2... Let me now go to the field, and glean ears of corn after him in whose sight I shall find grace.

glean– To gather what the reapers leave behind from their harvest. Not gather of the field but only what has been left or dropped.

Ruth realized she was entitled to only what the reapers left behind. By the grace of the Lord of the harvest, could glean in his field.

Chapter 2
V.1-2
NOTES

(1) V.1 N_____

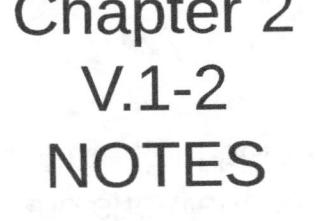

V.2 R_____ the M_____

(3)

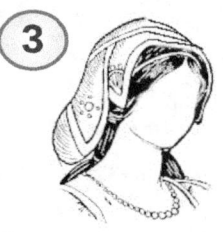

(5) V.2 Go, my d_____.

(4) V.2... Let me now go to the field, and g_____ ears of c_____ after him in whose sight I shall f_____ g_____.

(2) V.2 ...a k_____ of her h_____, a mighty man of w_____, of the family of E_____; and his name was B_____.

Chapter 2
V.3
GUIDE

Naomi

V.3
Boaz

V.3
1

V.3
2

Elimelech
(family member)

husband

RIP
Father

near kinsman

Ruth

husband

Mahlon
Eldest Son

Was not expecting to be in the field of Boaz. It was the providence of God that led her to his field.

V.3 And she went, and came, and gleaned in the field *after the reapers:* and *her hap* was to light on a part of the field belonging unto *Boaz,* who was of the *kindred of Elimelech.*

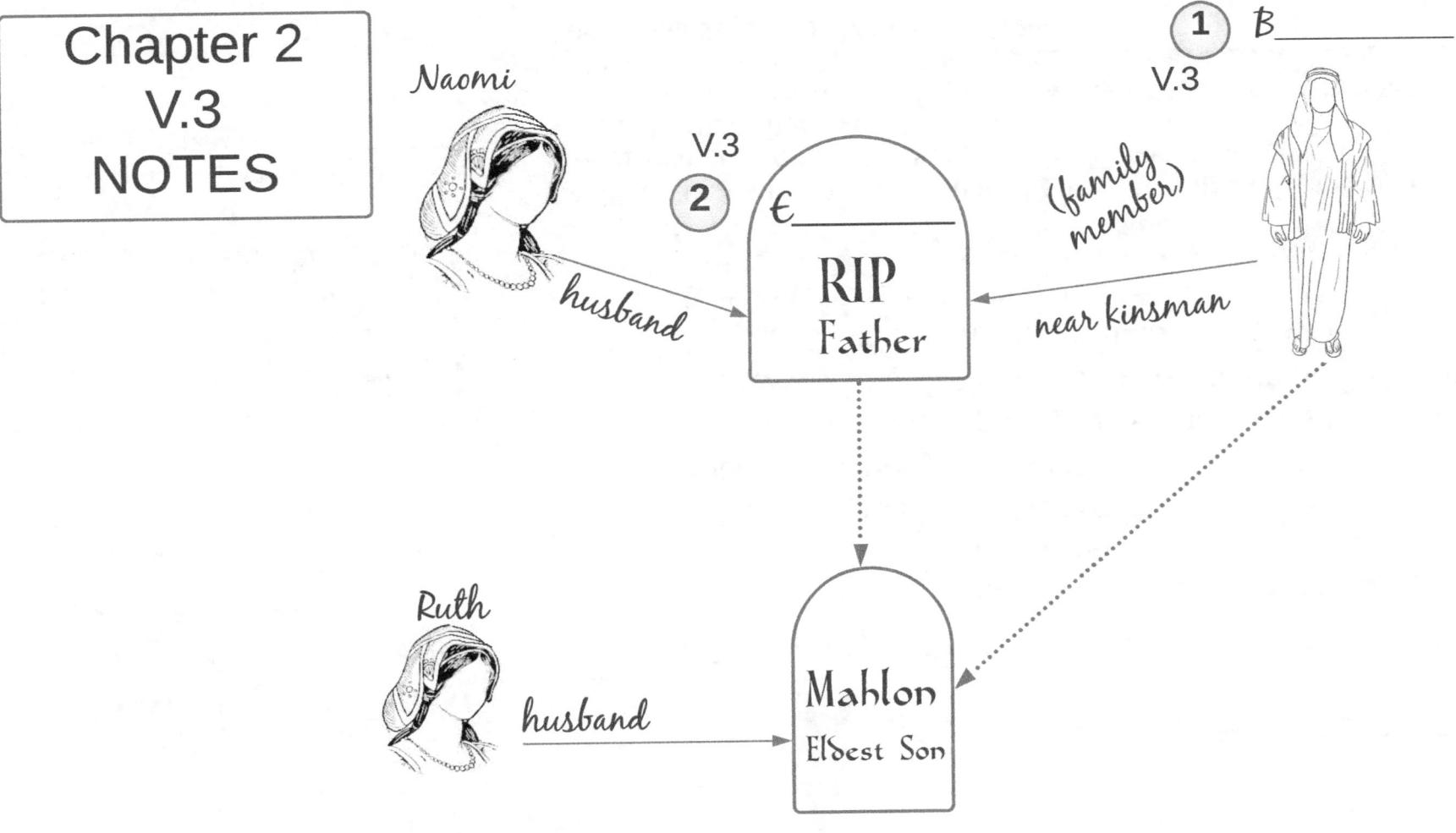

Chapter 2
V.3
NOTES

Naomi

Bible reference
V.3

1 B_____

(family member)

V.3
2 E_____

RIP
Father

husband

near kinsman

Ruth

husband

Mahlon
Eldest Son

V.3 And she went, and came, and gleaned in the field a_____ the r_____: and *her hap* was to light on a part of the field belonging unto B_____, who was of the k_____ *of* E_____.

Chapter 2
V.4-7
GUIDE

③ V. 4 The *LORD* be with you.

④ V. 4 The *Lord bless thee.*

①

V.4 Boaz

② *V.4 reapers*

⑥ V. 5 *Whose* damsel is this?

⑤ V. 5 *Servant*

Ruth

A stranger to the children of Israel.
(not a Jew)

⑦ V.6 It is the *Moabitish* damsel that came back with *Naomi* out of the country of *Moab*:
V.7 And she said, I pray you, let me *glean and gather after the reapers among the sheaves:* so she came, and hath *continued* even from the morning until now, that she *tarried a little* in the house.

stedfast

diligent in her work

God cares for the poor. Gleaning is a law that was made so the poor and strangers to Israel may support themselves.

The Old Testament Law of Gleaning

Leviticus 19:9 And <u>when ye reap the harvest of your land, thou shalt not wholly reap the corners of thy field, neither shalt thou gather the gleanings of thy harvest.</u>
Leviticus 19:10 And thou shalt not glean thy vineyard, neither shalt thou gather every grape of thy vineyard; <u>thou shalt leave them for the poor and stranger: I am the LORD your God.</u>

Chapter 2
V.4-7
NOTES

(4) V. 4 The L_____
b_____ t_____.

(3) V. 4 The L_____ be
w_____ y_____.

(1) V.4 B_____

(2) V.4
r_____

(5) V. 5 S_____

(6) V. 5 W_____
damsel is this?

Ruth

(7) V.6 It is the M_____ damsel that came back
with N_____ out of the country of M_____:
V.7 And she said, I pray you, let me g_____ and
g_____ a_____ the r_____ among
the s_____: so she came, and hath c_____
even from the morning until now, that she t_____ a
l_____ in the house.

Boaz

Naomi

V.10 Then she fell on her *face,* *and bowed herself to the ground,* and said unto him, *Why* have I *found grace* in thine eyes, that thou shouldest take knowledge of me, seeing I am a *stranger?*

She went out seeking grace.

Not an Israelite. She's a Moabite

V.8 Hearest thou not, my daughter? Go *not to glean in another field,* neither go from hence, but abide here fast by *my maidens:*

V.9 Let thine eyes be on the field that they do reap, and go thou after them: have I not charged the *young men* that they *shall not touch thee?* and when thou art *athirst, go unto the vessels, and drink of that which the young men have drawn.*

Boaz

Ruth

V.8 Hearest thou not, my daughter? Go n_____ to g_____ in a_____ f_____, neither go from hence, but abide here fast by my m_____:

V.9 Let thine eyes be on the field that they do reap, and go thou after them: have I not charged the young men that they shall not touch thee? and when thou art a_____, go unto the v_____, and d_____ of that which the y_____ m_____ have d_____.

V.10 Then she fell on her f_____, and b_____ h_____ to the g_____, and said unto him, W_____ have I f_____ g_____ in thine eyes, that thou shouldest take knowledge of me, seeing I am a stranger?

Ruth

Boaz

1

V.11 ...It hath *fully been shewed me,* all that thou hast done unto thy mother in law since the *death of thine husband:* and how thou hast left thy father and thy mother, and the *land of thy nativity,* and art come *unto a people* which thou knewest not heretofore.

V.12 The LORD *recompense thy work,* and a full reward be given thee of the LORD God of Israel, under whose *wings thou art come to trust.*

Matthew 23:37 ...<u>how often would I have gathered thy children together, even as a hen gathereth her chickens under her wings, and ye would not!</u>

But Ruth did!

2

V.13 ...Let me find *favour in thy sight,* my lord; for that thou hast *comforted me,* and for that thou hast spoken friendly unto *thine handmaid,* though I *be not like* unto one of thine handmaidens.

3 V. 14...At *mealtime* come thou hither, and *eat of the bread,* and dip thy *morsel in the vinegar.* And she sat beside the reapers: and *he reached her parched corn, and she did eat, and was suffieed,* and left.

Chapter 2 V.11-14 NOTES

Ruth

Boaz

(1)

V.11 ...It hath f_____ been s_____ m_____, all that thou hast done unto thy mother in law since the d_____ of t_____ h_____: and how thou hast left thy father and thy mother, and the l_____ of thy n_____, and art come *unto a* p_____ which thou knewest not heretofore.

V.12 The LORD r_____ *thy* w_____, and a full reward be given thee of the LORD God of Israel, under whose w_____ *thou* a_____ *come to* t_____.

(2) V.13 ...Let me find f_____ *in thy s*_____, my lord; for that thou hast c_____ m_____, and for that thou hast spoken friendly unto t_____ h_____, though I b____ n_____ l_____ unto one of thine handmaidens.

(3) V. 14...At *mealtime* come thou hither, and e_____ *of the* b_____, and dip thy m_____ *in the* v_____. And she sat beside the reapers: and *he* r_____ h____ p_____ c_____, and s_____ *did* e_____, and w_____ s_____, and left.

Chapter 2
V.15-16
GUIDE

① V. 15 *his young men*

Ruth

Boaz

Strangers in New Testament are called Gentiles. They are referred to as dogs.

Matthew 15:26 But he answered and said, It is not meet to take the <u>children's bread,</u> and to cast it to dogs.

children of Israel

Matthew 15:27 And she said, Truth, Lord: <u>yet the dogs eat of the crumbs which fall from their masters' table</u>.

strangers

law of gleaning

②

V. 15...Let her *glean even among the sheaves*, and reproach her not:

V.16 And let fall also some of *the handfuls of purpose for her,* and leave them, that she may *glean* them, and rebuke her not.

Ruth

① V. 15 h_____
y_____ m_____

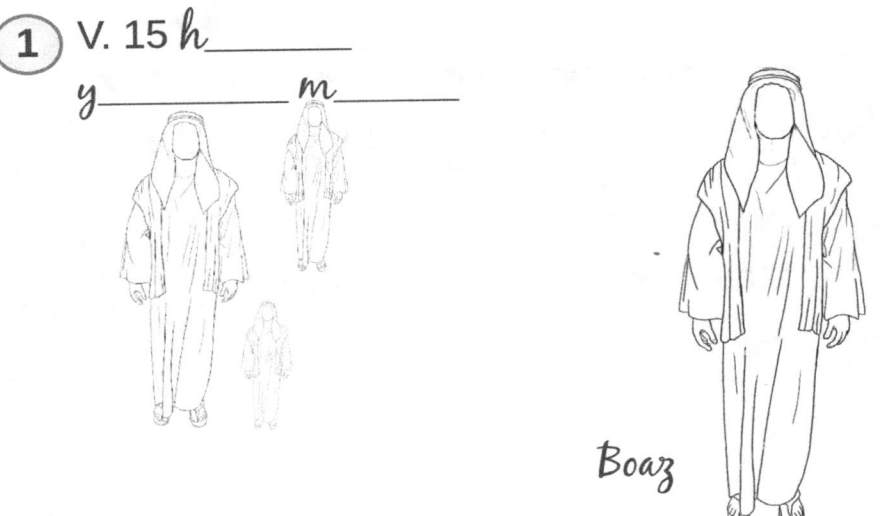

Boaz

②

V. 15...Let her g_____ even a_____ the s_____,
and r_____ her n_____:
V.16 And let fall also some of the h_____ of
p_____ for h_____, and leave them, that she may
g_____ them, and r_____ her n_____.

② V. 19 *Where* hast thou gleaned to day? and where wroughtest thou? *blessed be he* that did *take knowledge of thee.*

worked

③ V. 19 The man's name with whom I wrought to day is *Boaz.*

Naomi

Ruth

①

V.17 So she gleaned in the field *until even,* and *beat out* that she had gleaned: and it was about an *ephah of barley. (about a bushel)*

Naomi

V.18 And she took it up, and *went into the city*: and *her mother in law* saw what she had gleaned: and she *brought forth,* and *gave to her* that she had reserved *after she was sufficed.*

...and thine house. Boaz not only provided for Ruth but for Naomi as well.

② V. 19 W_____ hast thou gleaned to day? and where wroughtest thou? b_____ be h_____ that did t_____ k_____ of t_____.

③ V. 19 The man's name with whom I wrought to day is B_____.

Ruth

Naomi

①

V.17 So she gleaned in the field u_____ e_____, and b_____ o_____ that she had gleaned: and it was about an e_____ of b_____.

V.18 And she took it up, and w_____ into the c_____: and h_____ m_____ in l_____ saw what she had gleaned: and she b_____ f_____, and g_____ to h_____ that she had reserved a_____ s_____ was s_____.

Naomi

Ruth

Chapter 2
V.20-22
GUIDE

Will provide for Ruth and Naomi, as well as raise up a child so Elimelech's name will not put out.

1 V.20 ...*Blessed be he of the LORD,* who hath not left off his kindness *to the living and to the dead.* And Naomi said unto her, The *man is near of kin unto us, one of our next kinsmen.*

provided for her protection.

2 V. 21 He said unto me also, Thou shalt keep fast by *my young men,* until they have *ended all my harvest.*

Boaz is a picture of Jesus

Matthew 9:38 Pray ye therefore <u>the Lord of the harvest,</u> that he will send forth labourers into his harvest.

3 V.22 it is good, my daughter, that thou go out *with his maidens,* that they meet thee not in any other field.

Jesus

Ruth   Naomi

1

V.20 ...B_____ be h____ of the
L_____, who hath not left off his kindness
to the l_____ and to the
d_____. And Naomi said unto her, The
m_____ is n_____ of k_____ unto u_____,
o_____ of our n_____ k_____.

2

V. 21 He said unto me also, Thou shalt
keep fast by m_____ y_____
m_____, until they have e_____
a_____ m_____ h_____.

3 V.22 it is good, my daughter, that thou go
out w_____ h_____ m_____,
that they meet thee not in any other field.

Naomi

Ruth

V.23 So she kept fast by the *maidens of Boaz* to glean unto the *end of barley harvest and of wheat harvest;* and *dwelt with her mother in law.*

springtime   autumn

Naomi

Ruth

V.23 So she k_____ f_____ by the m_____ of B_____ to glean unto the end of b_____ h_____ and of w_____ h_____; and dwelt with her m_____ in l____.

Read Chapter 3

Psalm 119:105 Thy word is a lamp unto my feet, and a light unto my path.

Chapter 3
V.1-5
GUIDE

John 14:15 If ye love me, keep my commandments.

Ruth

Ruth's love for Naomi is clearly seen with her trust and obedience

2

V.5 ... All that thou sayest unto me I will do.

(Under Jewish law the nearest kinsman is obligated to redeem Naomi and Ruth.)

Winnowing is tossing the grain up into the air to separate the chaff. The chaff is the worthless waste that is blown into the wind.

Naomi

By law Boaz should redeem Naomi. She is the wife of his kin, Elimelech. But Naomi's love for Ruth is clearly seen when she seeks rest and the well being of Ruth over herself.

1

V.1 ...My daughter, shall I not seek rest for thee, that it may be well with thee?

V.2 And now is not Boaz of our kindred, with whose maidens thou wast?

Behold, he winnoweth barley to night in the threshingfloor.

V.3 Wash thyself therefore, and anoint thee, and put thy raiment upon thee, and get thee down to the floor: but make not thyself known unto the man, until he shall have done eating and drinking.

V.4 And it shall be, when he lieth down, that thou shalt mark the place where he shall lie, and thou shalt go in, and uncover his feet, and lay thee down; and he will tell thee what thou shalt do.

Ruth

(2)

V.5 ... A_____ that thou s_____ unto me __ w_____ d____.

Naomi

(1)

V.1 ...My daughter, shall I not s_____ r_____ for t_____, that it may be w_____ with t_____?

V.2 And now is n_____ B_____ of o_____ k_____, with whose maidens thou wast?

Behold, he w_____ b_____ to night in the t_____.

V.3 W_____ t_____ therefore, and a_____ t_____, and put thy r_____ upon t_____, and get thee down to the floor: but make not thyself known unto the man, until he shall have done eating and drinking.

V.4 And it shall be, when he lieth down, that thou shalt mark the place where he shall lie, and thou shalt go in, and u_____ his f_____, and l____ thee d_____; and he will t_____ t_____ what thou s_____ do.

1 V.6 And she went down unto the floor, and *did according to all* that her mother in law bade her.

generic for grain.

2 V.7 And when Boaz had eaten and drunk, and his heart was merry, he went to lie down at the end of the heap of *corn:* and she came softly, and *uncovered his feet, and laid her down.*

It was his feet she uncovered. Not his nakedness. It was an act of humility.

3 V.8 And it came to pass *at midnight,* that the man *was afraid,* and turned himself: and, behold, a *woman lay at his feet.*

startled him because he was not expecting her.

5 Ruth

Boaz

V.9...I am *Ruth thine handmaid: spread therefore thy skirt over thine handmaid; for thou art a near kinsman.*

4 V.9 ...*Who art thou*

The first time they met, Boaz said unto her...

Ruth 2:12 The LORD <u>recompense thy work, and a full reward be given thee</u> of the LORD God of Israel, <u>under whose wings thou art come to trust.</u>

Ruth is asking Boaz, as her near kinsman, to spread his wings over her because she has come to trust in him.

6 V.10 And he said, *Blessed be thou* of the LORD, my daughter: for thou hast *shewed more kindness in the latter end than at the beginning,* inasmuch as thou followedst *not young men, whether poor or rich.*

Ruth was young and beautiful. She could have turned back with Orpah to remarry and start a new life. Instead, she refused to leave Naomi. Now she is obedient and seeks to marry an older man that most young people would not. She did not give in to the lusts and riches of this world.

Ruth

(1) V.6 And she went down unto the floor, and d_____
a_____ to a_____ that her mother in law bade her.

(2) V.7 And when Boaz had eaten and drunk, and his heart was merry, he went to lie down at the end of the heap of _corn:_ and she came softly, and u_____ his f_____, and l_____ her d_____.

(3) V.8 And it came to pass _at m_____, that the man was a_____, and turned himself: and, behold, a w_____ l_____ at his f_____.

(4)

Boaz

V.9 ...W_____ art t_____

(5)

V.9...I am R_____
t_____
h_____:
s_____ _therefore thy_
s_____over
t_____
h_____; _for thou_
_art a n_____
k_____.

(6) V.10 And he said, B_____ _be thou_ of the LORD, my daughter: for thou hast s_____ more k_____ in the l_____ e_____ _than at the_ b_____, inasmuch as thou followedst n_____y_____ m_____, _whether_ p_____ _or_ r_____.

Ruth

Boaz

V.11 And now, my daughter, fear not; I will do to thee *all that thou requirest*: for all the *city of my people* doth know that thou art *a virtuous woman*.

Proverbs 31:10 Who can find a *virtuous woman*? for her price is far above rubies.

Proverbs 31:11 The *heart of her husband* doth safely trust in her, so that he shall have no need of spoil.

Proverbs 31:12 She will *do him good* and not evil all the days of *her life*.

Proverbs 31:13 She seeketh wool, and flax, and *worketh willingly with her hands*.

Proverbs 31:14 She is like the merchants' ships; she *bringeth her food from afar*.

Proverbs 31:15 She riseth also while it is yet night, and *giveth meat to her household*, and a portion to her maidens.

Proverbs 31:16 She considereth a field, and buyeth it: with the fruit of her hands she planteth a vineyard.

Proverbs 31:17 She *girdeth her loins with strength*, and strengtheneth *her arms*.

Proverbs 31:18 She perceiveth that her merchandise is good: her *candle goeth not out by night*.

Proverbs 31:19 She layeth her hands to the spindle, and *her hands* hold the distaff.

Proverbs 31:20 She stretcheth out her hand to the poor; yea, she reacheth forth her hands to the needy.

Proverbs 31:21 She is not afraid of the snow *for her household*: for all her household are clothed with scarlet.

Proverbs 31:22 She maketh herself coverings of tapestry; her clothing is silk and purple.

Proverbs 31:23 Her *husband is known in the gates*, when he sitteth among the elders of the land.

Proverbs 31:24 She maketh fine linen, and selleth it; and delivereth girdles unto the merchant.

Proverbs 31:25 Strength and honour are her clothing; and *she shall rejoice in time to come*.

Proverbs 31:26 She openeth her mouth *with wisdom*; and in her tongue is the *law of kindness*.

Proverbs 31:27 She looketh well to the ways of her household, and *eateth not the bread of idleness*.

Proverbs 31:28 Her *children arise up*, and call her blessed; *her husband also*, and he praiseth her.

Proverbs 31:29 Many daughters have done *virtuously*, but thou excellest them all.

Proverbs 31:30 Favour is deceitful, and beauty is vain: but a woman that *feareth the LORD*, she shall be praised.

Proverbs 31:31 Give her of the fruit of her hands; and *let her own works praise her in the gates*.

All these things are true of Ruth.

Ruth

Boaz

V.11 And now, my daughter, fear not; I will do to thee all that thou requirest: for all the city of my people doth know that thou art a v_____ woman.

Proverbs 31:10 Who can find a v_____ woman? for her price is far above rubies.
Proverbs 31:11 The h_____ of her h_____ doth safely trust in her, so that he shall have no need of spoil.
Proverbs 31:12 She will do h_____ g_____ and not evil all the days of h_____ l_____.
Proverbs 31:13 She seeketh wool, and flax, and w_____ willingly with h_____ h_____.
Proverbs 31:14 She is like the merchants' ships; she b_____ her f_____ from a_____.
Proverbs 31:15 She riseth also while it is yet night, and giveth meat to h_____ h_____, and a portion to her maidens.
Proverbs 31:16 She considereth a field, and buyeth it: with the fruit of her hands she planteth a vineyard.
Proverbs 31:17 She g_____ her loins with s_____, and strengtheneth her a_____.
Proverbs 31:18 She perceiveth that her merchandise is good: her c_____ g_____ not out by n_____.
Proverbs 31:19 She layeth her hands to the spindle, and her hands hold the distaff.
Proverbs 31:20 She stretcheth out her hand to the poor; yea, she reacheth forth her hands to the needy.
Proverbs 31:21 She is not afraid of the snow for h_____ h_____: for all her household are clothed with scarlet.
Proverbs 31:22 She maketh herself coverings of tapestry; her clothing is silk and purple.
Proverbs 31:23 Her h_____ is known in the g_____, when he sitteth among the elders of the land.
Proverbs 31:24 She maketh fine linen, and selleth it; and delivereth girdles unto the merchant.
Proverbs 31:25 Strength and honour are her clothing; and she shall r_____ in t_____ t___ c_____.
Proverbs 31:26 She openeth her mouth with w_____; and in her tongue is the law of k_____.
Proverbs 31:27 She looketh well to the ways of her household, and e_____ not the b_____ of i_____.
Proverbs 31:28 Her c_____ a_____ up, and call her blessed; her h_____ also, and he praiseth her.
Proverbs 31:29 Many daughters have done v_____, but thou excellest them all.
Proverbs 31:30 Favour is deceitful, and beauty is vain: but a woman that f_____ the L_____, she shall be praised.
Proverbs 31:31 Give her of the fruit of her hands; and let her o_____ w_____ praise her in the g_____.

Ruth

Boaz

Leviticus 25:25   Naomi had came back to Bethlehem poor and was selling land that belonged to her deceased husband, Elimelech. The land needed to be redeemed by a near kinsman to keep it in the family.

See next page on Kinsman-Redeemer

① V.12 And now it is true that *I am thy near kinsman:* howbeit *there is a kinsman nearer than I.*

② V.13 Tarry this night, and it shall be in the morning, that if he will perform unto thee the part of a kinsman, well; *let him do the kinsman's part:* but if he will not do the part of a kinsman to thee, *then will I do the part of a kinsman to thee,* as the LORD liveth: lie down until the morning.

③ V.14 And she lay at his feet *until the morning:* and she rose up before one could know another.

④ V. 14 Let it not be known that *a woman came* into the floor.

⑤ V.15 Bring *the vail* that thou hast upon thee, and hold it. And when she held it, *he measured six measures of barley,* and laid it on her: .

⑥ V. 15...and she went *into the city*

Ruth

Boaz

(1) V.12 And now it is true that ___ a___ t_____ n_____ k_____: howbeit *there is a* k_____ n_____ t_____ ____.

(2) V.13 Tarry this night, and it shall be in the morning, that if he will perform unto thee the part of a kinsman, well; *let* h_____ *do the* k_____ p_____: but i___ he will n_____ do the part of a kinsman to thee, t_____ w_____ ____ d____ *the part of a kinsman to thee,* as the LORD liveth: lie down until the morning.

(3)

V.14 And she lay at his feet u_____ *the* m_____: and she rose up before one could know another.

(4) V. 14 Let it not be known that *a* w_____ c_____ into the floor.

(5) V.15 Bring *the* v_____ that thou hast upon thee, and hold it. And when she held it, *he measured* s_____ m_____ *of* b_____, and laid it on her: .

(6) V. 15...and she went *into the* c_____

Chapter 3 Kinsman-Redeemer GUIDE

...the part of a kinsman... Ruth 3:13

Buy back, ransom or bring back from captivity.

1. Redeem property his brother sold as a result of poverty

Leviticus 25:25 If thy brother be *waxen poor*, and hath sold away some of his possession, and if any of *his kin* come to *redeem it*, then shall he redeem that which *his brother sold.*

2. Marry the widow of a deceased brother to continue his name

Deuteronomy 25:5 If brethren dwell together, and one of them die, and have no child, the wife of the dead shall not marry without unto a stranger: her *husband's brother shall go in unto her*, and *take her to him to wife*, and perform the duty of an husband's brother unto her.

Deuteronomy 25:6 And it shall be, that *the firstborn* which she beareth shall succeed in the *name of his brother* which is dead, *that his name be not put out of Israel.*

...the part of a kinsman... Ruth 3:13

Boaz

Buy back, ransom or bring back from captivity.

1. Redeem property his brother sold as a result of poverty

Leviticus 25:25 If thy brother be w_____ p_____, and hath sold away some of his possession, and if any of h_____ k_____ come to r_____ it, then shall he redeem that which h_____ b_____ s_____.

2. Marry the widow of a deceased brother to continue his name

Deuteronomy 25:5 If brethren dwell together, and one of them die, and have no child, the wife of the dead shall not marry without unto a stranger: her h_____ b_____ s_____ go in u_____ h_____, and t_____ h_____ to h_____ to w_____, and perform the duty of an husband's brother unto her.
Deuteronomy 25:6 And it shall be, that the f_____ which she beareth shall succeed in the n_____ of h_____ b_____ which is dead, t_____ his n_____ be n_____ p_____ out of I_____.

Naomi

It is not that she didn't recognize Ruth. Was she still the same Ruth as when she left?

Ruth

1 V.16 ...Who art thou, *my daughter?*

2 V. 16...And *she told her all* that the man had done to her.

3 V.17 And she said, These *six measures of barley* gave he me; for he said to me, Go *not empty* unto thy mother in law.

4 V.18 ...*Sit still,* my daughter, until thou know how the matter will fall: *for the man will not be in rest,* until he have *finished the thing this day.*

Naomi

Ruth

1

V.16 ...Who art thou, m_____ d_____?

2

V. 16...And *she* t_____
h_____ a_____ that the man
had done to her.

3 V.17 And she said, These _____ m_____
of b_____ gave he me; for he said to me,
Go *not* e_____ unto thy mother in law.

4 V.18 ...S_____ s_____, my daughter, until thou know
how the matter will fall: *for the* m_____ *will* n____ *be in*
r_____, until he have f_____ *the* t_____
this day.

Read Chapter 4

*John 1:14 And the Word was made flesh, and dwelt among us,
(and we beheld his glory, the glory as of the only begotten of
the Father,) full of grace and truth.*

(2) kinsman who was a closer relative than Boaz. He is called a kinsman redeemer.

V. 1...the *kinsman* of whom Boaz spake *came by*

(1) V.1 Then went *Boaz* up to the *gate*, and *sat* him down there:

(4) V.1 And he turned aside, and *sat down*.

(3) V.1 *Ho*, such a one! turn aside, *sit down* here.

(5)

V.2 And he took *ten* men of the *elders of the city*, and said, Sit ye down here. And they *sat down*.

(2)

V. 1...the
k_____ of
whom Boaz
spake c_____
b_____

(4)

V.1 And he turned
aside, and s_____
d_____.

(1) V.1 Then went B_____ up
to the g_____, and
s_____ him down there:

(3)

V.1 _____, such a one!
turn aside, s_____
d_____ here.

(5)

V.2 And he took t_____
men of the e_____ of
the c_____, and said, Sit
ye down here. And they
s_____ d_____.

1 V.3 And he said unto the *kinsman*, Naomi, that is come again out of the country of Moab, *selleth a parcel of land*, which was *our brother Elimelech's:*

Boaz

When an Israelite family through poverty must sell their land, a near kinsman is to redeem it (buy it back) so that it does not leave the family.

Leviticus 25:24 And in all the land of your possession ye shall grant a redemption for the land.
Leviticus 25:25 If thy brother be waxen poor, and hath sold away some of his possession, and if any of his kin come to redeem it, then shall he redeem that which his brother sold.

kinsman

2 V.4 And I thought to advertise thee, saying, Buy it before the inhabitants, and before the elders of my people. *If thou wilt redeem it, redeem it:* but if thou wilt not redeem it, then tell me, that I may know: for there is none to redeem it beside thee; and *I am after thee.*

3

V.4 And he said, *I will redeem it.*

10 elders of the city

Boaz

1 V.3 And he said unto the k_____, N_____, that is come again out of the country of Moab, s_____ a p_____ of l_____, which was o_____ b_____ E_____:

kinsman

2 V.4 And I thought to advertise thee, saying, Buy it before the inhabitants, and before the elders of my people. *If thou* w_____ r_____ *it,* r_____ *it:* but if thou wilt not redeem it, then tell me, that I may know: for there is none to redeem it beside thee; and _____ a_____ a_____ t_____.

10 elders of the city

3 V.4 And he said, _____ w_____ r_____ i_____.

10 elders of the city

Boaz

ELIMELECH
FATHER

MAHLON
ELDEST SON

near kinsman

Because of Naomi's age, she could not bare another son to raise up to Elimelech's name. Therefore, he must redeem Ruth, the wife of the eldest son.

1

V.5 Then said Boaz, What day thou buyest the field of the hand of Naomi, thou must buy it also of Ruth the Moabitess, the wife of the dead, to raise up the name of the dead upon his inheritance.

Deuteronomy 25:5 If brethren dwell together, and one of them die, and have no child, the wife of the dead shall not marry without unto a stranger: <u>her husband's brother shall go in unto her, and take her to him to wife, and perform the duty of an husband's brother unto her.</u>

2

V.6 ... I cannot redeem it for myself, lest I mar mine own inheritance: redeem thou my right to thyself; for I cannot redeem it.

Chapter 4
V. 5-6
NOTES

10 elders of the city

Boaz

ELIMELECH
FATHER

MAHLON
ELDEST SON

1

V.5 Then s_____ B_____, What day thou b_____ the f_____ of the h_____ of N_____, thou must buy it also of R_____ the M_____, the wife of the dead, to r_____ up the n_____ of the d_____ upon his inheritance.

near kinsman

2

V.6 ... I cannot redeem it for myself, lest I mar mine own inheritance: r_____ thou my r_____ to t_____; for I c_____ r_____ it.

near kinsman

Boaz

The near kinsman was not able to unloose the latchet of the shoe of Boaz. He must pluck off his own shoe.

gives it to Boaz

plucks off his shoe

10 elders of the city (witnesses)

V.7 Now this was the manner in former time in Israel concerning redeeming and concerning changing, for to confirm all things; a man plucked off his shoe, and gave it to his neighbour: and this was a testimony in Israel.

V.8 Therefore the kinsman said unto Boaz, Buy it for thee. So he drew off his shoe.

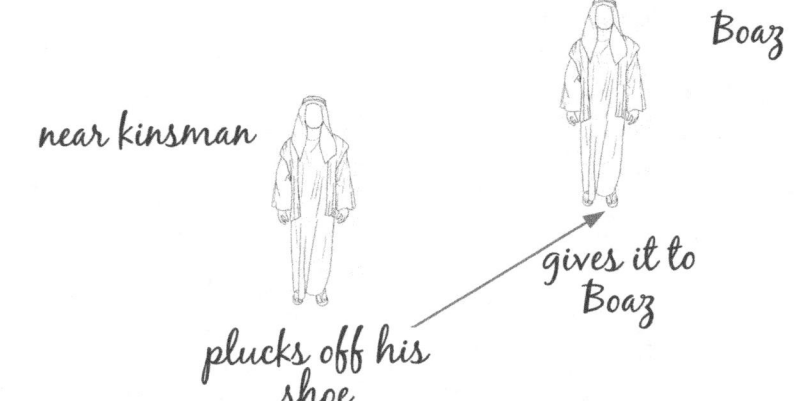

near kinsman

Boaz

gives it to
Boaz

plucks off his
shoe

10 elders of the
city (witnesses)

V.7 Now this was the manner in former time in Israel concerning
r_____ and concerning c_____, for to confirm all things; a
man p_____ o_____ h_____ s_____, and gave it to his
neighbour: and this was a t_____ in I_____.
V.8 Therefore the kinsman said unto Boaz, B_____ it f_____
t_____. So he drew off h_____ s_____.

Boaz

10 elders of the city

witnesses

1 V.9 *Ye are witnesses* this day, that I have *bought all* that was *Elimelech's*, and all that was *Chilion's and Mahlon's, of the hand of Naomi.*

2 V.10 Moreover *Ruth the Moabitess, the wife of Mahlon, have I purchased to be my wife, to raise up the name of the dead upon his inheritance,* that the name of the dead be not cut off from among his brethren, and from the gate of his place: ye are witnesses this day.

Boaz

10 elders of the city

witnesses

1

V.9 Ye are w_____ this day, that I have b_____ a_____ that was E_____, and a_____ that was C_____ and M_____, of the h_____ of N_____.

2 V.10 Moreover R_____ the M_____, the w_____ of M_____, have _____ p_____ to be m_____ w_____, to r_____ u____ the n_____ of the d_____ u_____ his i_____, that the name of the dead be not cut off from among his brethren, and from the gate of his place: ye are witnesses this day.

V.11 And *all the people* that were in the gate, and the elders, said, We are witnesses. The LORD make the woman that is come into thine house like *Rachel and like Leah,* which two did build *the house of Israel:* and do thou worthily in Ephratah, and *be famous in Bethlehem:*

Abraham

Isaac

Broke forth first over his twin brother Genesis 28:26

Esau (father of Edomites)

Jacob (God named Israel)

Leah

Rachael

Boaz

The 12 Tribes of Israel

All the people and the elders

Genesis 38:29 And it came to pass, as he drew back his hand, that, behold, his brother came out: and she said, How hast thou broken forth? this breach be upon thee: therefore his name was called Pharez.

Tamar

1. Reuben
2. Simeon
3. Levi
4. Judah

5, Dan
6. Naphtali
11. Joseph
12. Benjamin

Pharez   Zarah

7. Gad
8. Asher
9. Issachar
10. Zebulun

Broke forth first over his twin brother

V.11 And all the p_____that were in the gate, and the e_____, said, We are witnesses. The LORD make the woman that is come into thine house l_____ R_____ and l_____ L_____, which two did build the h_____ of I_____: and do thou worthily in Ephratah, and be f_____ in B_____:

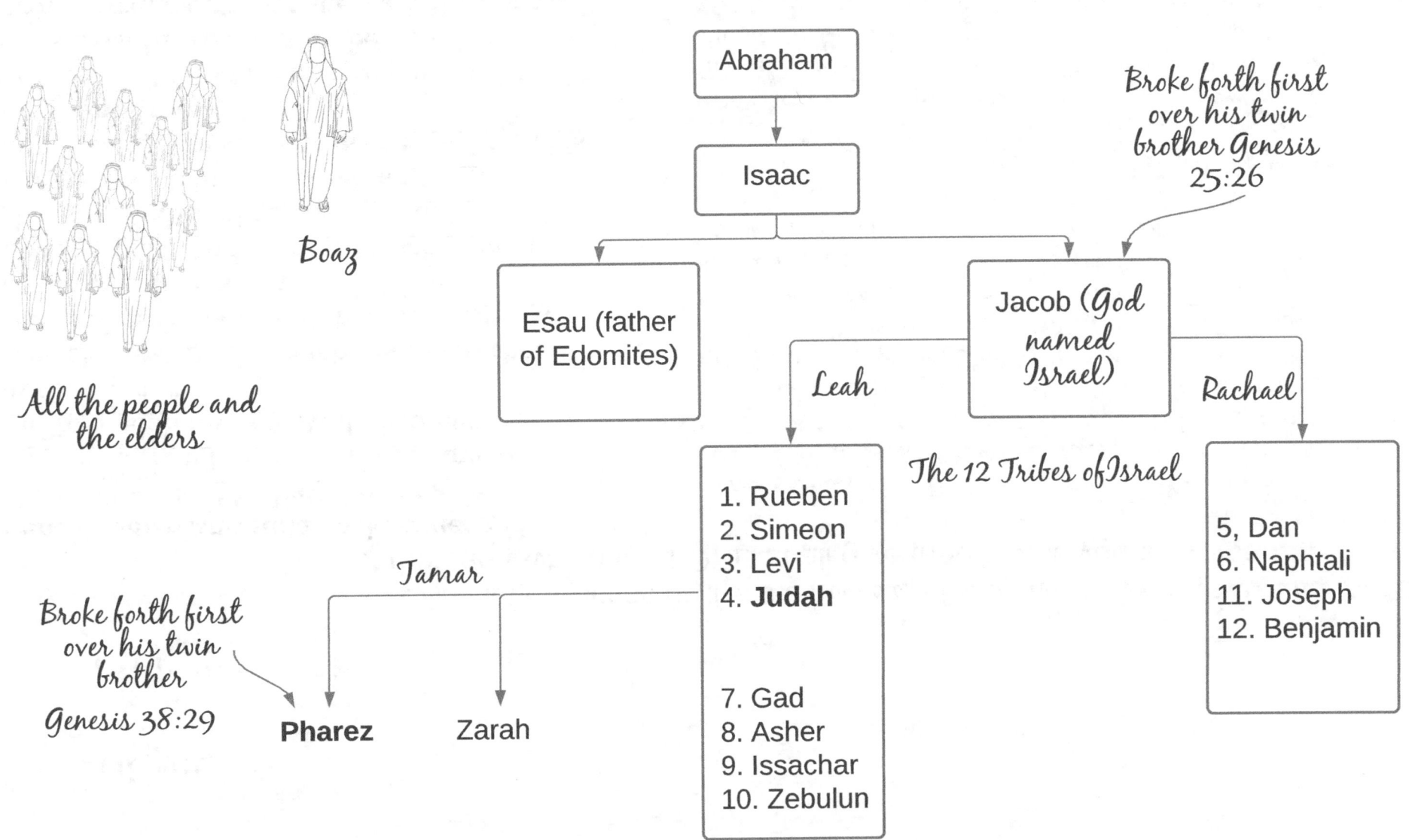

All the people and the elders

Boaz

Abraham

Isaac

Broke forth first over his twin brother Genesis 25:26

Esau (father of Edomites)

Jacob (God named Israel)

Leah

Rachael

The 12 Tribes of Israel

1. Rueben
2. Simeon
3. Levi
4. **Judah**

7. Gad
8. Asher
9. Issachar
10. Zebulun

5, Dan
6. Naphtali
11. Joseph
12. Benjamin

Tamar

Broke forth first over his twin brother Genesis 38:29

Pharez   Zarah

Boaz   Ruth

Tamar

V.12 And let thy house be like the house of Pharez, whom Tamar bare unto Judah, of the seed which the LORD shall give thee of this young woman.

Genesis 38:26 And Judah acknowledged them, and said, She hath been more righteous than I; because that I gave her not to Shelah my son. And he knew her again no more.

Genesis 38:27 And it came to pass in the time of her travail, that, behold, twins were in her womb. Same as Jacob & Esau

Genesis 38:28 And it came to pass, when she travailed, that the one put out his hand: and the midwife took and bound upon his hand a scarlet thread, saying, This came out first.

Genesis 38:29 And it came to pass, as he drew back his hand, that, behold, his brother came out: and she said, How hast thou broken forth? this breach be upon thee: therefore his name was called Pharez. Same as Jacob and Esau (Genesis 25:26)

Genesis 38:30 And afterward came out his brother, that had the scarlet thread upon his hand: and his name was called Zarah.

Tamar's husband died and she was left a widow. According to Jewish law, her husband's brother was supposed to marry her and raise up children in her husband's name. Judah, her father in law, promised her if she waited for Shelah, her husband's brother, to become old enough he would give him to her for a husband. Judah broke his promise. So Tamar deceived Judah and played a harlot. Through this act of whoredom, Pharez was conceived.

Pharez was a bastard and could not enter into the congregation of the Lord for 10 generations by Jewish law. Deut. 23:2 He had a twin brother named Zarah, who should have been born first. They tied a scarlet thread upon Zarah's hand so they knew which came out first. But Pharez broke forth first. Same as Jacob and Esau. Jacob was blessed because he also broke forth ahead of Esau.

See Chapter 4:18-22.

Boaz   *Ruth*

Tamar

V.12 And let thy house be like the *house of P*_____, *whom J*_____ *bare unto J*_____, of the seed which the LORD shall give thee of this young woman.

Genesis 38:26 And Judah acknowledged them, and said, <u>She hath been more righteous than I; because that I gave her not to Shelah my son.</u> And he knew her again no more.

Genesis 38:27 And it came to pass in the time of her travail, that, behold, <u>twins were in her womb.</u> *Same as Jacob & Esau*

Genesis 38:28 <u>And it came to pass, when she travailed, that the one put out his hand: and the midwife took and bound upon his hand a scarlet thread, saying, This came out first.</u>

Genesis 38:29 And it came to pass, as he drew back his hand, that, behold, his brother came out: and she said, <u>How hast thou broken forth? this breach be upon thee: therefore his name was called Pharez.</u> *Same as Jacob and Esau (Genesis 25:26)*

Genesis 38:30 And <u>afterward</u> came out his brother, that had the scarlet thread upon his hand: and his name was called <u>Zarah.</u>

Ruth

Boaz

1 V.13 *So Boaz took Ruth, and she was his wife:* and when he went in unto her, the LORD gave her conception, and *she bare a son.*

the women

Naomi

Naomi said the Lord had afflicted her and she was coming back empty. She came back with more....for Ruth was better to her than 7 sons. God provided her with a kinsman to restore her life and nourish her in her old age.

10 elders of the city

2 V.14 And the women said unto Naomi, Blessed be the LORD, which hath *not left thee this day without a kinsman, that his name may be famous in Israel.*

3 V.15 And he shall be unto thee *a restorer of thy life,* and a *nourisher of thine old age:* for thy daughter in law, which loveth thee, which is *better to thee than seven sons, hath born him.*

Ruth

Boaz

1 V.13 So B_____ took R_____, and she was his w_____:
and when he went in unto her, the LORD gave her conception,
and she b_____ a s_____.

the women   Naomi

10 elders of the city

2 V.14 And the women said unto Naomi, Blessed be the LORD, which hath not
left thee this day w_____ a k_____, that his name may
be f_____ in I_____.

3 V.15 And he shall be unto thee a r_____ of thy l_____, and a
n_____ of thine o_____ a_____: for thy daughter in law, which
loveth thee, which is better to thee than s_____ s_____, hath born him.

Naomi

The Women

① V.16 And *Naomi* took the *child*,
and laid it in *her bosom*, and
became *nurse* unto it.

② V.17 And the *women her neighbours gave it a name,*
saying, There is *a son born to Naomi;* and they called
his name *Obed:* he is the *father of Jesse, the father of
David.*

Chapter 4
V. 16-17
NOTES

Naomi

The Women

① V.16 And N_____ took the c_____,
and laid it in h_____ b_____, and
became n_____ unto it.

② V.17 And the w_____ her n_____ gave
it a n_____, saying, There is a s_____ b_____ to
N_____; and they called his name O_____: he is the
father of J_____, the father of D_____.

V.18 Now these are the generations of Pharez: *Pharez* begat *Hezron*,

V.19 And Hezron begat *Ram*, and Ram begat *Amminadab*,

V.20 And Amminadab begat *Nahshon*, and Nahshon begat *Salmon*,

V.21 And Salmon begat *Boaz*, and Boaz begat *Obed*,

V.22 And Obed begat *Jesse*, and Jesse begat *David*.

The mother of Boaz was the harlot named Rahab who hid the 2 Israelite spies that had came to spy out the land of Jericho. She confessed that the God of Israel was God in heaven above and on earth. (Joshua 2)

He married a woman who is a stranger to Israel but had forsaken all for the God of Israel.

Pharez
1

Father was Judah
Mother was Tamar
Jesus Christ is the
Lion from the Tribe
of Judah

Hezron
2

Ram
3

Amminadab
4

Nahshon
5

Rahab (mother)

Entered into the
congregation of the
Lord. Became King
of Israel

Salmon
6

Boaz
7

Ruth became the great
grandmother of King David.

Obed
8

Jesse
9

King David
10th

Chapter 4
V. 18-22
NOTES

V.18 Now these are the generations of Pharez: P_____ begat H_____,
V.19 And Hezron begat R_____, and Ram begat A_____,
V.20 And Amminadab begat N_____, and Nahshon begat
S_____,
V.21 And Salmon begat B_____, and Boaz begat O_____,
V.22 And Obed begat J_____, and Jesse begat D_____.

P_____
1

Hezron
2

Ram
3

Amminadab
4

Nahshon
5

Salmon
6

B_____
7

Obed
8

Jesse
9

King D_____
10th

10th Generation GUIDE

Pharez →

Moab →

<u>Deuteronomy 23:2</u> A *bastard* shall not enter into the congregation of the LORD; even to *his tenth generation* shall he not enter into the congregation of the LORD.

<u>Deuteronomy 23:3</u> An Ammonite or *Moabite* shall not enter into the congregation of the LORD; even to their *tenth generation* shall they not enter into the congregation of the LORD for ever:

We don't know Ruth's moabite lineage but Lot and Abraham was of the same generation.
Moab was Lot's son from incest.

Pharez/Boaz

1. **Pharez (bastard)**
2. Hezron
3. Ram
4. Aminnadab
5. Nashon
6. Salmon
7. **Boaz** (Ruth)
8. Obed
9. Jesse
10. **King David**

King David was the 10th generation from Pharez (Bastard) so he could enter into the congregation of the Lord.

Moab/Ruth

1. Abraham-**Lot** *Genesis 13:1*
2. Isaac-**Moab (bastard)** (1) *Genesis 19:37-37*
3. *Jacob (2)*
4. Judah (3)
5. Pharez (4)
6. Hezron (5)
7. Ram (6)
8. Aminnadab (7)
9. Nashon (8)
10. Salmon (9)
11. Boaz **(Ruth) (10th)**
12. Obed
13. Jesse
14. **King David**

Ruth was the 10th generation from Moab so she could enter into the congregation of the Lord.

Matthew 1:17 So all the generations from Abraham to David are fourteen generations;

Pharez/Boaz Deuteronomy 23:2 A b_____ shall not enter into the congregation of the LORD; even to *his* t_____ g_____ shall he not enter into the congregation of the LORD.

Moab/Ruth Deuteronomy 23:3 An Ammonite or *M*_____ shall not enter into the congregation of the LORD; even to their t_____ g_____ shall they not enter into the congregation of the LORD for ever:

We don't know Ruth's moabite lineage but the generations of Lot would be the same number as the generations of Abraham. Moab was Lot's son from incest.

Generations of Boaz

1. **Pharez (bastard)**
2. Hezron
3. Ram
4. Aminnadab
5. Nashon
6. Salmon
___. **Boaz** (Ruth)
8. Obed
9. Jesse
___. **King David**

Generations of Ruth

1. Abraham-**Lot** *Genesis 13:1*
2. Isaac-**Moab (bastard)** (1) *Genesis 19:37-37*
3. Jacob (2)
4. Judah (3)
5. Pharez (4)
6. Hezron (5)
7. Ram (6)
8. Aminnadab (7)
9. Nashon (8)
10. Salmon (9)
11. Boaz **(Ruth)** (____th)
12. Obed
13. Jesse
____ King David

Matthew 1:17 So all the generations from Abraham to David are fourteen generations;

Some of the names are spelled differently because the Old Testament is written in Hebrew. The New Testament names are written in Greek.

Matthew 1:1 The book of the generation of Jesus Christ, the son of David, the son of Abraham.

Matthew 1:2 Abraham begat Isaac; and Isaac begat Jacob; and Jacob begat Judas and his brethren;

Matthew 1:3 And Judas begat Phares and Zara of Thamar; and Phares begat Esrom; and Esrom begat Aram;

Matthew 1:4 And Aram begat Aminadab; and Aminadab begat Naasson; and Naasson begat Salmon;

Matthew 1:5 And Salmon begat Booz of Rachab; and Booz begat Obed of Ruth; and Obed begat Jesse;

Matthew 1:6 And Jesse begat David the king; and David the king begat Solomon of her that had been the wife of Urias;

Matthew 1:7 And Solomon begat Roboam; and Roboam begat Abia; and Abia begat Asa;

Matthew 1:8 And Asa begat Josaphat; and Josaphat begat Joram; and Joram begat Ozias;

Matthew 1:9 And Ozias begat Joatham; and Joatham begat Achaz; and Achaz begat Ezekias;

Matthew 1:10 And Ezekias begat Manasses; and Manasses begat Amon; and Amon begat Josias;

Matthew 1:11 And Josias begat Jechonias and his brethren, about the time they were carried away to Babylon:

Matthew 1:12 And after they were brought to Babylon, Jechonias begat Salathiel; and Salathiel begat Zorobabel;

Matthew 1:13 And Zorobabel begat Abiud; and Abiud begat Eliakim; and Eliakim begat Azor;

Matthew 1:14 And Azor begat Sadoc; and Sadoc begat Achim; and Achim begat Eliud;

Matthew 1:15 And Eliud begat Eleazar; and Eleazar begat Matthan; and Matthan begat Jacob;

Matthew 1:16 And Jacob begat Joseph the husband of Mary, of whom was born Jesus, who is called Christ.

Some of the names are spelled differently because the Old Testament are written in Hebrew. The New Testament names are written in Greek.

Matthew 1:1 The book of the *generation of* J_____ C_____, *the son of* D_____, *the son of* A_____.

Matthew 1:2 Abraham begat Isaac; and Isaac begat Jacob; and J_____ *begat* J_____ and his brethren;

Matthew 1:3 And Judas begat P_____ and Zara of J_____; and Phares begat Esrom; and Esrom begat Aram;

Matthew 1:4 And Aram begat Aminadab; and Aminadab begat Naasson; and Naasson begat Salmon;

Matthew 1:5 And Salmon begat B_____ *of* R_____; *and Booz begat* O_____ *of* R_____; *and Obed begat* J_____;

Matthew 1:6 And *Jesse begat* D_____ *the* k_____; and David the king begat Solomon of her that had been the wife of Urias;

Matthew 1:7 And Solomon begat Roboam; and Roboam begat Abia; and Abia begat Asa;

Matthew 1:8 And Asa begat Josaphat; and Josaphat begat Joram; and Joram begat Ozias;

Matthew 1:9 And Ozias begat Joatham; and Joatham begat Achaz; and Achaz begat Ezekias;

Matthew 1:10 And Ezekias begat Manasses; and Manasses begat Amon; and Amon begat Josias;

Matthew 1:11 And Josias begat Jechonias and his brethren, about the time they were carried away to Babylon:

Matthew 1:12 And after they were brought to Babylon, Jechonias begat Salathiel; and Salathiel begat Zorobabel;

Matthew 1:13 And Zorobabel begat Abiud; and Abiud begat Eliakim; and Eliakim begat Azor;

Matthew 1:14 And Azor begat Sadoc; and Sadoc begat Achim; and Achim begat Eliud;

Matthew 1:15 And Eliud begat Eleazar; and Eleazar begat Matthan; and Matthan begat Jacob;

Matthew 1:16 And J_____ *begat* J_____ *the husband of* M_____, of whom was born J_____, *who is* c_____ C_____.

REDEEMED by Fanny Crosby

1 Redeemed, how I love to proclaim it!
Redeemed by the blood of the Lamb;
Redeemed through His infinite mercy,
His child, and forever, I am.

CHORUS:
Redeemed, redeemed,
Redeemed by the blood of the Lamb;
Redeemed, how I love to proclaim it!
His child, and forever, I am.

2 I think of my blessed Redeemer,
I think of Him all the day long;
I sing, for I cannot be silent;
His love is the theme of my song. [Refrain]

3 I know I shall see in His beauty
The King in whose law I delight,
Who lovingly guardeth my footsteps,
And giveth me songs in the night. [Refrain]

Prophecy of the Nation of Israel and the Church

Not only does the Book of Ruth give us historical knowledge of the geneaology of Christ and God's providence in the first coming of the Messiah, it also contains the prophecy of how the Church and the Nation of Israel will be brought into one fold in the end times.

Hosea 12:10 I have also spoken by the prophets, and I have multiplied visions, and <u>used similitudes</u>, by the ministry of the prophets.

similitudes means uncountable similiarities.
Such as patterns and shadows

Read Chapter 1

Psalm 119:103 How sweet are thy words unto my taste! yea, sweeter than honey to my mouth!

Were not doing what was right in God's eyes but right in their own eyes, which was evil in the sight of the Lord.

Judges 17:6 In those days there was no king in Israel<u>, but every man did that which was right in his own eyes.</u>

(hunger) no bread in the land -symbolic for lack of the Word of God (The bread of life).

V.1 Now it came to pass in the days when the judges ruled, that there was a famine in the land. And a certain man of Bethlehemjudah went to sojourn in the country of Moab, he, and his wife, and his two sons.

Israel

Birthplace of Christ (The Bread of Life)

When he made the decision to walk away from God's provision his family was affected also.

sojourn—to live or dwell in a place as a temporary resident.

Only meant to walk away for a short while, but sin will always keep you longer than you meant to stay. His sons spent much of their life in a land where a false god was worshipped instead of the God of Israel.

Mediterranean Sea.

Dor

Taanach

Sochoh

Jordan River

Gibeon

Jerusalem

Bethlehem

Dead Sea

Gath

Judah

Moab

Ammon

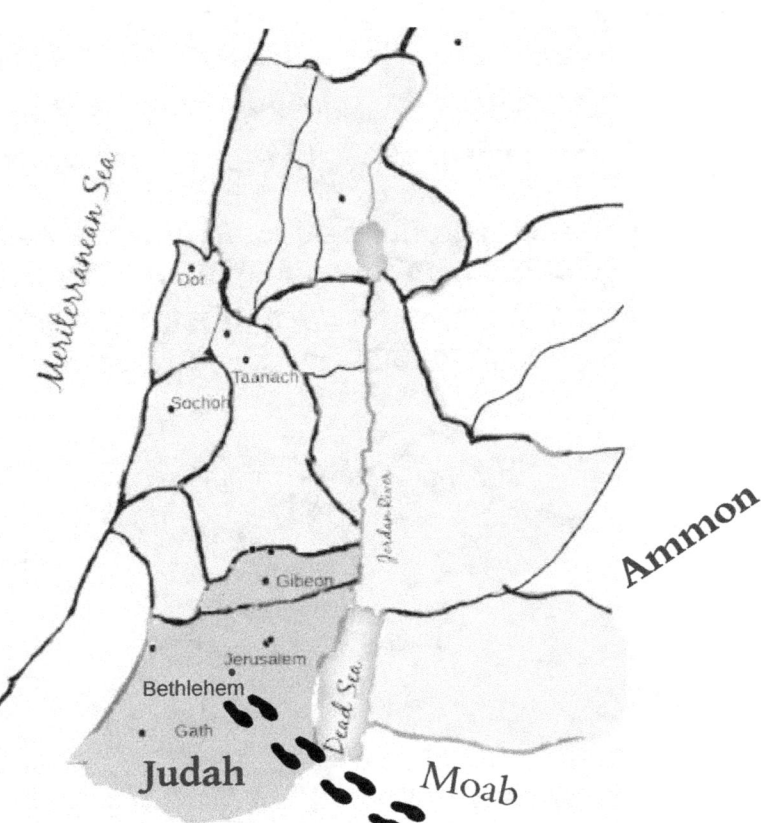

V.1 Now it came to pass in the days when the j_____ ruled, that there was a f_____ in t_____ l_____. And a certain man of B_____ went to s_____ in the country of Moab, h____, and h_____ w_____, and h_____ t_____ s_____.

Gentile-anyone who is not a Jew

Gentile nation

Moabites

V.1 Now it came to pass in the days when the judges ruled, that there was a famine in the land. And a certain man of Bethlehemjudah went to sojourn in the *country of Moab*, he, and his wife, and his two sons.

Moabites worshipped a false God called Chemosh.

2 Kings 23:13 and for *Chemosh the abomination of the Moabites,* **and for Milcom the abomination of the children of Ammon, did the king defile.**

Chemosh was worshipped with child sacrifice.

2 Kings 3:26 And <u>when the</u> *king of Moab* <u>saw that the battle was too sore for him,</u> he took with him seven hundred men that drew swords, to break through even unto the king of Edom: but they could not.

2 Kings 3:27 <u>Then he took his</u> *eldest son* <u>that should have</u> *reigned in his stead,* <u>and</u> *offered him for a burnt offering* <u>upon the wall.</u> And there was great indignation against Israel: and they departed from him, and returned to their own land.

If Ruth would have turned back, the same could have happened to Obed, her eldest son who was in the lineage of King David (which led to the King of Kings) who would reign over Israel.

Left the Promised Land went to a cruel godless nation looking for bread. This same nation refused bread to the Israelites when they were leaving Egypt.

Mediterranean Sea
Dor
Taanach
Socho
Gibeon
Jordan River
Jerusalem
Bethlehem
Dead Sea
Gath
Judah
Moab
Ammon

Deuteronomy 23:3 An <u>Ammonite or</u> *Moabite* <u>shall not enter into the congregation of the LORD; even to their</u> *tenth* <u>generation</u> shall they not enter into the congregation of the LORD for ever:
Deuteronomy 23:4 <u>Because they met you</u> *not* with *bread* and with *water* <u>in the way, when ye came forth</u> *out of Egypt;* <u>and because they hired against thee Balaam the son of Beor of Pethor of Mesopotamia, to curse thee.</u>

Moabites

V.1 Now it came to pass in the days when the judges ruled, that there was a famine in the land. And a certain man of Bethlehemjudah went to sojourn in the c_____ of M_____, he, and his wife, and his two sons.

2 Kings 23:13 and for C_____ the a_____ of the M_____, and for Milcom the abomination of the children of Ammon, did the king defile.

2 Kings 3:26 And when the k_____ of M_____ saw that the battle was too sore for him, he took with him seven hundred men that drew swords, to break through even unto the king of Edom: but they could not.

2 Kings 3:27 Then he took his e_____ s_____ that should have r_____ in his stead, and o_____ h_____ for a b_____ o_____ upon the wall. And there was great indignation against Israel: and they departed from him, and returned to their own land.

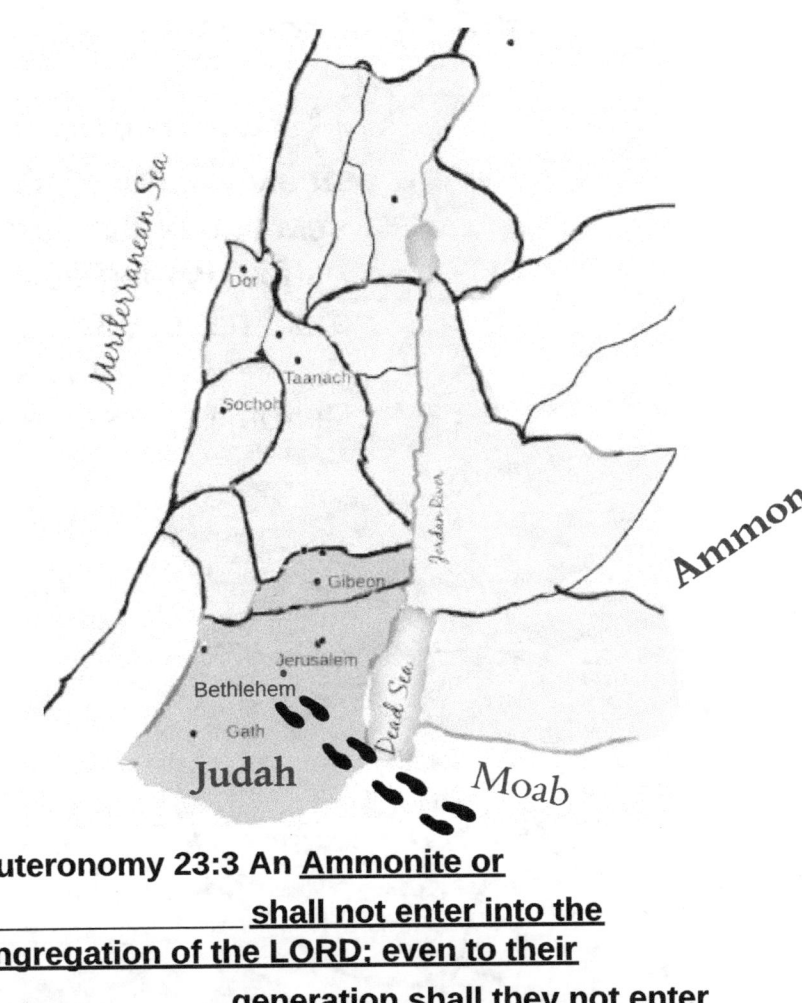

Deuteronomy 23:3 An Ammonite or M_____ shall not enter into the congregation of the LORD; even to their t_____ generation shall they not enter into the congregation of the LORD for ever: **Deuteronomy 23:4** Because they met you n_____ with b_____ and with w_____ in the way, when ye came forth out of E_____; and because they hired against thee Balaam the son of Beor of Pethor of Mesopotamia, to curse thee.

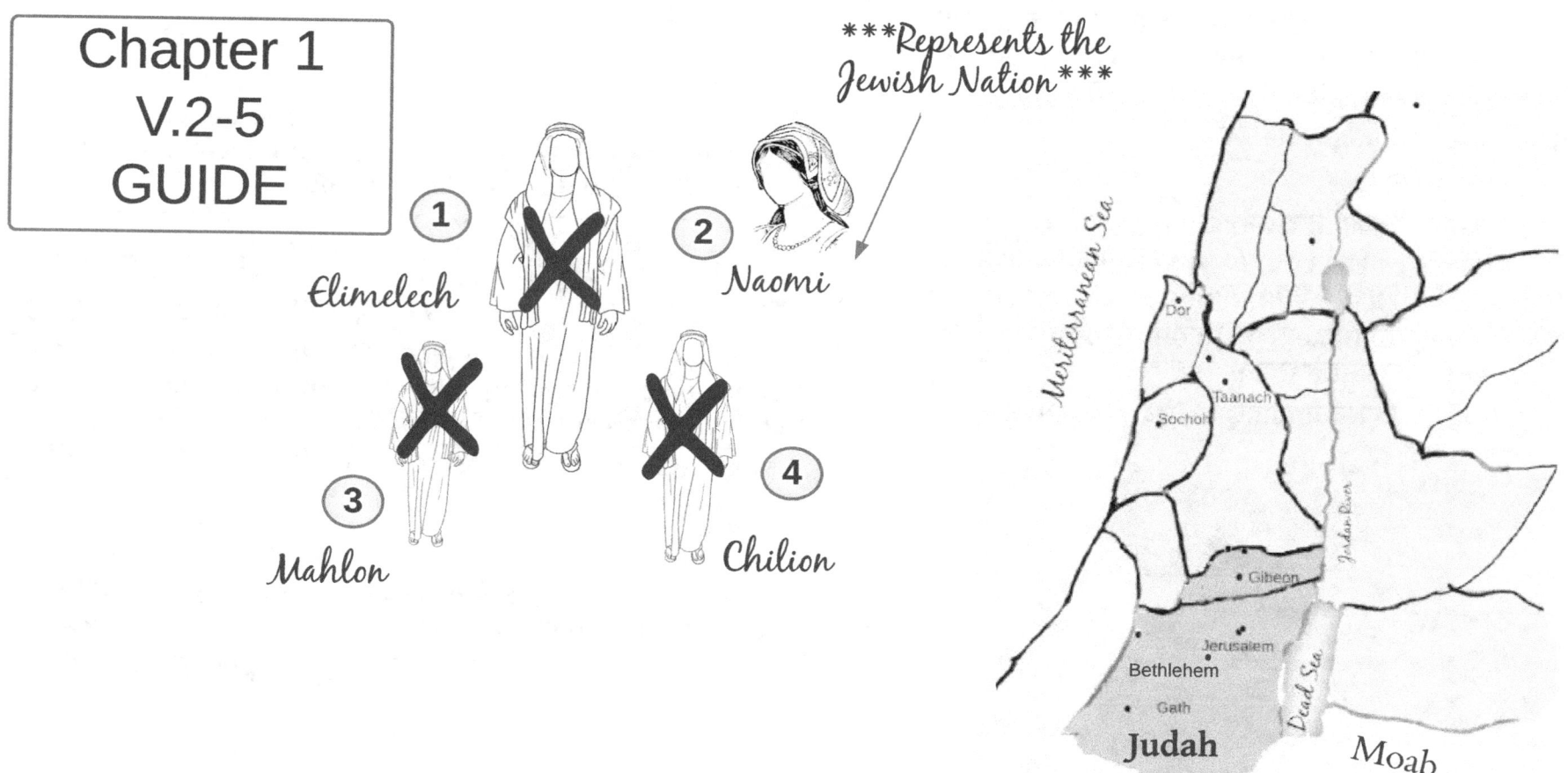

Chapter 1 V.2-5 GUIDE

① Elimelech

② Naomi

Represents the Jewish Nation

③ Mahlon

④ Chilion

Mediterranean Sea

Dor

Taanach

Sochoh

Gibeon

Jerusalem
Bethlehem

Gath

Judah

Dead Sea

Jordan River

Moab

V.2 And the name of the man was Elimelech, and the name of his wife Naomi, and the name of his two sons Mahlon and Chilion, Ephrathites of Bethlehemjudah. And they came into the country of Moab, and continued there.
V.3 And Elimelech Naomi's husband died; and she was left, and her two sons.
V.4 And they took them wives of the women of Moab; the name of the one was Orpah, and the name of the other Ruth: and they dwelled there about ten years.
V.5 And Mahlon and Chilion died also both of them; and *the woman was left of her two sons and her husband.*

God always leaves a remnant of His people.

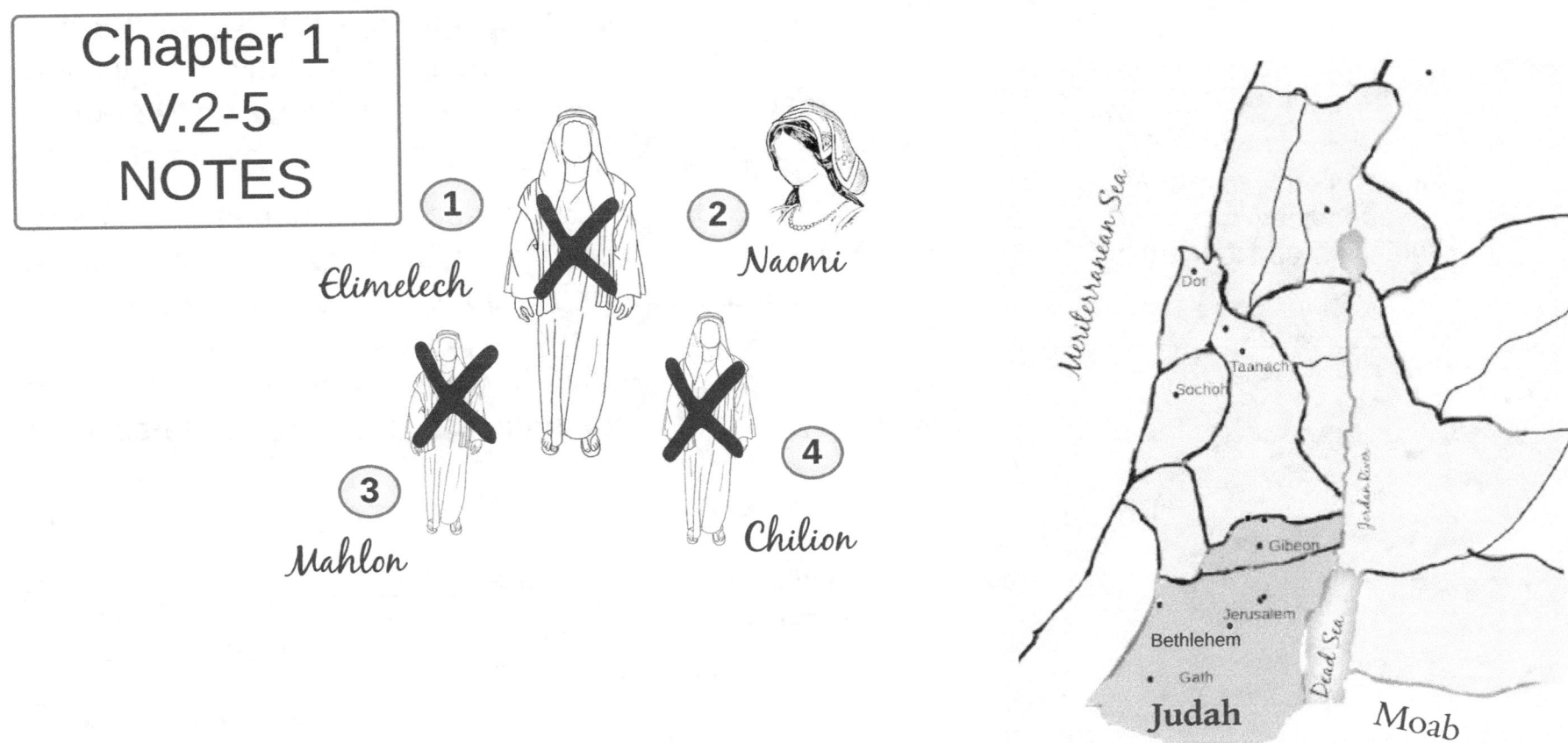

V.2 And the name of the man was Elimelech, and the name of his wife Naomi, and the name of his two sons Mahlon and Chilion, Ephrathites of Bethlehemjudah. And they came into the country of Moab, and continued there.
V.3 And Elimelech Naomi's husband died; and she was left, and her two sons.
V.4 And they took them wives of the women of Moab; the name of the one was Orpah, and the name of the other Ruth: and they dwelled there about ten years.
V.5 And Mahlon and Chilion died also both of them; and the w_____ was l_____ of her two s_____ and her h_____.

When Naomi went to find bread. (Jesus) Ruth and Orpah had a chance to follow. What we do affects other.

John 6:35 And Jesus said unto them, I am the bread of life:

V.6 Then she arose with her daughters in law, that she might return from the country of Moab: for she had heard in the country of Moab how that the LORD had visited his people in giving them bread.

Symbolic of when the Bread of Life was manifested in the flesh.

Luke 1:68 Blessed be the Lord God of Israel; for he <u>hath</u> visited **and** redeemed <u>his people,</u>

At the same time she returns from wickedness, she returns unto the blessings of God.

V.7 Wherefore she went forth out of the place where she was, and her two daughters in law with her; and they went on the way to return unto the land of Judah.

V.8 And Naomi said unto her two daughters in law, Go, return each to her mother's house: the LORD deal kindly with you, as ye have dealt with the dead, and with me.

V.9 The LORD grant you that ye may find rest, each of you in the house of her husband. Then she kissed them; and they lifted up their voice, and wept.

John 3:29 He that hath the bride is the bridegroom:

Mediterranean Sea

Dor

Taanach

Sochoh

Gibeon

Jerusalem

Bethlehem

Gath

Judah

Jordan River

Dead Sea

Moab

Orpah

Ruth

Matthew 11:28 <u>Come unto me,</u> all ye that labour and are heavy laden, and <u>I will give you</u> rest.

Rest is found in Jesus,

The husband is symbolic of Jesus

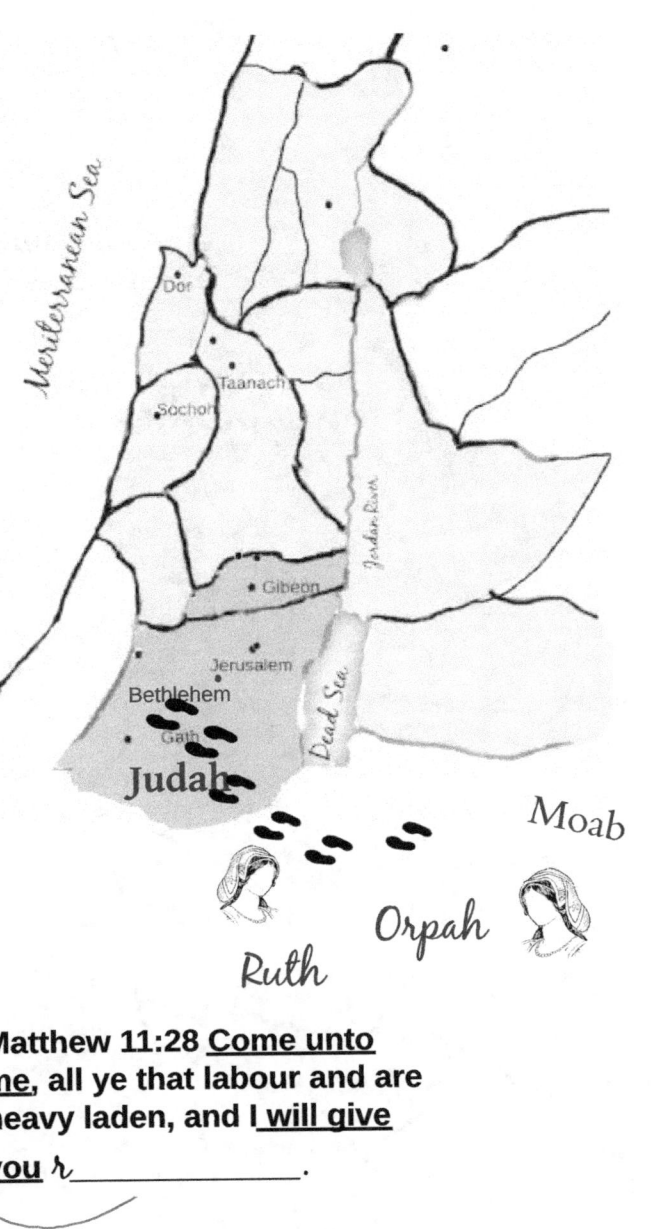

V.6 Then she arose with her daughters in law, that she might r_____ f_____ the country of M_____: for she had heard in the country of Moab how that the LORD had v_____ his people in giving them *bread.*

Luke 1:68 Blessed be the Lord God of Israel; for he hath v_____ and *redeemed* his people.

V.7 Wherefore she went forth out of the place where she was, and her two daughters in law with her; and they went on the way to r_____ u_____ the land of _____.

V.8 And Naomi said unto her two daughters in law, Go, return each to her mother's house: the LORD deal kindly with you, as ye have dealt with the dead, and with me.

V.9 The LORD grant you that ye may find *rest,* each of you in the h_____ of her h_____. Then she kissed them; and they lifted up their voice, and wept.

Matthew 11:28 Come unto me, all ye that labour and are heavy laden, and I will give you r_____.

John 3:29 He that hath the bride is *the b*_____:

*** *Naomi representing the Jewish nation will lead the Gentiles to the redeemer, even though, the Jews rejected Him themselves.*

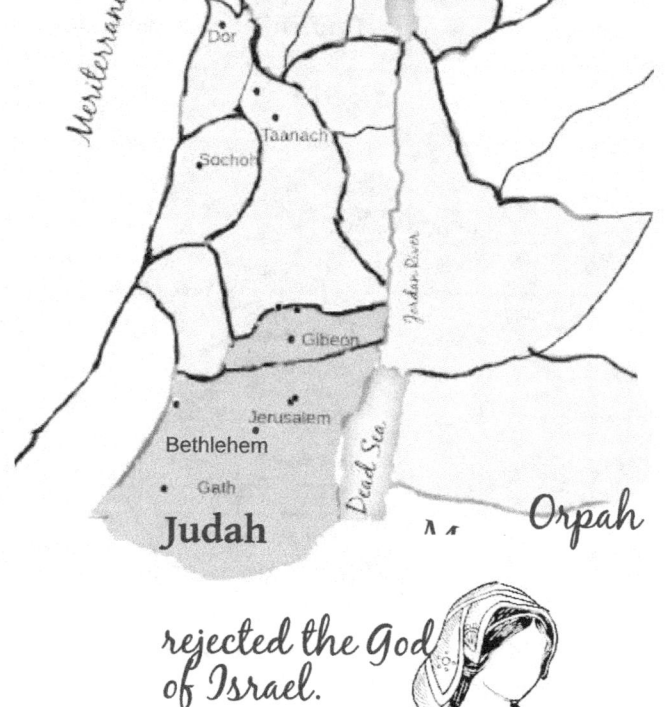

V.10 And they said unto her, Surely *we* will *return with thee* unto *thy people.*

V.11 And Naomi said, *Turn again*, my daughters: *why* will ye go with me? are there yet any more sons in my womb, that they may be your husbands?

V.12 *Turn again*, my daughters, *go your way*; for I am too old to have an husband. If I should say, I have hope, if I should have an husband also to night, and should also bear sons;

V.13 *Would ye* tarry for them till they were grown? *would ye stay* for them from having husbands? nay, my daughters; for it grieveth me much for your sakes that the hand of the LORD is gone out against me.

Orpah

rejected the God of Israel.

Romans 11:25 For I would not, brethren, that ye should be ignorant of this mystery, lest ye should be wise in your own conceits; that blindness in part is happened to Israel, until the *fulness* **of the** *Gentiles* **be come in.**

Naomi was separated from Israel until after Mahlon had died.
The Jewish nation was scattered until the Gentile Bride (church) was ripe. (fulness)

V.10 And they said unto her, Surely w_____ will r_____ w_____ t_____ unto t_____ p_____.

V.11 And Naomi said, T_____ a_____, my daughters: w_____ will ye go with me? are there yet any more sons in my womb, that they may be your husbands?

V.12 T_____ a_____, my daughters, g___ y_____ w_____; for I am too old to have an husband. If I should say, I have hope, if I should have an husband also to night, and should also bear sons;

V.13 W_____ y___ t_____ for them till they were grown? w_____ y___ s_____ for them from having husbands? nay, my daughters; for it grieveth me much for your sakes that the hand of the LORD is gone out against me.

Orpah

rejected the God of Israel.

Romans 11:25 For I would not, brethren, that ye should be ignorant of this mystery, lest ye should be wise in your own conceits; that blindness in part is happened to Israel, until the f_____ of the G_____ be come in.

Naomi was separated from Israel until after Mahlon had died.
The Jewish nation was scattered until the Gentile Bride (church) was ripe. (fulness)

*** Naomi representing the Jewish nation will lead the Gentiles to the redeemer, even though, the Jews rejected Him themselves.

V.14 And they lifted up their voice, and wept again: and Orpah kissed her mother in law; but Ruth clave unto her.

V.15 And she said, Behold, thy sister in law is gone back unto her people, and unto her gods: return thou after thy sister in law.

Naomi's bitterness discouraged Orpah so that she never found the God of Israel.

She went back unto her gods. Moab was part of the same wilderness that the childern of Israel had to cross in order to get to the Promised Land. As many of the Israelites were not allowed to leave the wilderness because of their unbelief, so is this true of Orpah.

Hebrews 3:17 But with whom was he grieved forty years? was it not with them that had sinned, whose carcases fell in the wilderness?

Hebrews 3:18 And to whom sware he that they should not enter into his rest, but to them that believed not?

Hebrews 3:19 So we see that they could not enter in because of unbelief.

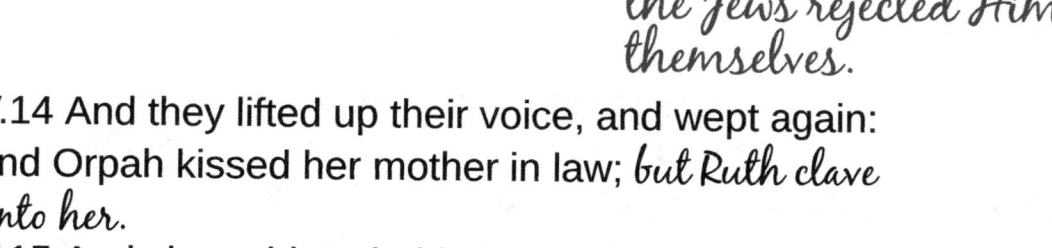

*** Orpah represents gentiles who did not believe in the God of Israel.

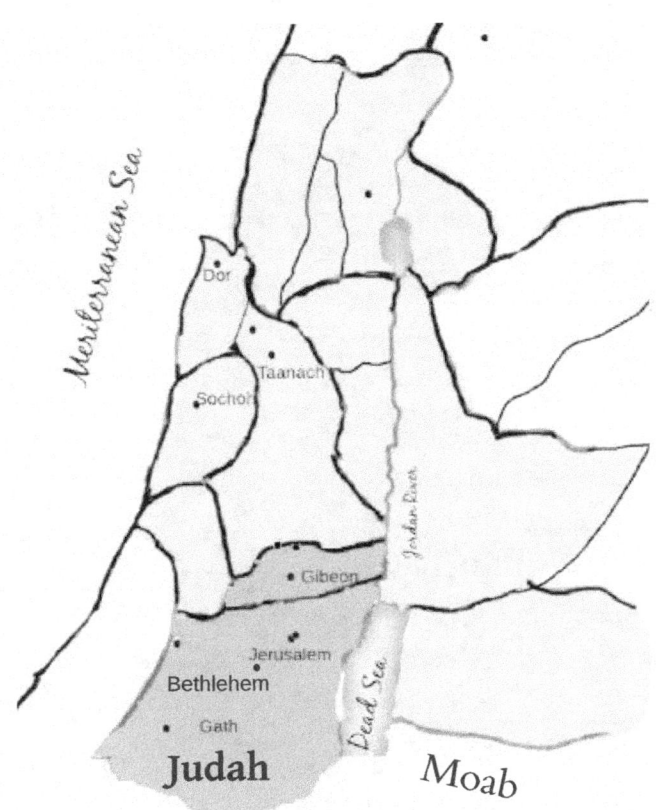

V.14 And they lifted up their voice, and wept again: and Orpah kissed her mother in law; b_____
R_____ c_____ unto her.
V.15 And she said, Behold, thy sister in law is
g_____ b_____ unto her p_____, and unto
her g_____: return thou after thy sister in law.

Hebrews 3:17 But with whom was he grieved forty years? was it not with them that had sinned, whose carcases fell in the wilderness?

Hebrews 3:18 And to whom sware <u>he that they should</u> n_____ e_____ <u>into his</u>
r_____, <u>but to them that</u> b_____ n_____?

Hebrews 3:19 <u>So we see that they could not enter in because of</u> u_____.

The gentile bride
(The Church)

Ruth

Ruth representing the Gentile bride had a willing heart to accept the God of Israel and His ways.

Jeremiah 29:13 And ye shall *seek me,* **and** *find me,* **when ye shall** *search* **for me with all your** *heart.*

V.16 for whither thou goest, *I will go;* and where thou lodgest, *I will lodge:* thy people shall be *my people,* and thy God *my God:*

V.17 Where thou diest, *will I die,* and there *will I be buried:* the LORD do so to me, and more also, if ought but *death part thee and me.*

marriage vows

Ruth forsook all for Naomi, her people and the God of Israel.

Matthew 19:29 And *every one* **that hath** *forsaken houses,* **or** *brethren,* **or** *sisters,* **or** *father,* **or** *mother,* **or** *wife,* **or** *children,* **or** *lands,* **for** *my name's sake,* **shall receive an hundredfold, and shall inherit everlasting life.**

Mediterranean Sea

Dor

Taanach

Socho

Gibeon

Jordan River

Jerusalem

Bethlehem

Dead Sea

Gath

Judah

Moab

Ruth

Jeremiah 29:13 And ye shall s_____ m____, and f_____ m_____, when ye shall s_____ for me with all your h_____.

V.16 for whither thou goest, *I* w_____ g____; and where thou lodgest, *I* w_____ l_____: thy people shall be *my* p_____, and thy God *my* g_____:

V.17 Where thou diest, w_____*I* d_____, and there w_____ *I be* b_____: the LORD do so to me, and more also, if ought but d_____ p_____ t_____ *and* m_____.

Matthew 19:29 And *e*_____ *o*_____ that hath f_____ h_____, or f_____, or s_____, or f_____, or m_____, or w_____, or c_____, or l_____, for m____ n_____ s_____, **shall receive an hundredfold, and shall inherit everlasting life.**

Luke 9:62 And Jesus said unto him, No man, having put his hand to the plough, and <u>looking back,</u> is fit for the kingdom of God.

Unlike Orpah

V.18 When she saw that she was *stedfastly minded* to go with her, then she left speaking unto her.
V.19 So they two went until they came to Bethlehem. And it came to pass, when they were come to Bethlehem, that all the city was moved about them, and they said, *Is this Naomi?*

Didn't recognize her after she had been out in the world.

V.20 And she said unto them, Call me not Naomi, call me Mara: for *the Almighty hath dealt very bitterly with me.*
V.21 *I went out full* and the LORD hath *brought me home again empty*: why then call ye me Naomi, seeing the LORD hath *testified against* me, and the Almighty hath afflicted me?

Naomi's family had disobeyed God when the famine was in the land. They left Israel.

Mediterranean Sea.

Dor
Taanach
Sochoh
Gibeon
Jordan River
Jerusalem
Bethlehem
Gath
Dead Sea
Judah
Moab

Naomi

V.18 When she saw that she was s_____
m_____ to go with her, then she left
speaking unto her.
V.19 So they two went until they came to Bethlehem.
And it came to pass, when they were come to
Bethlehem, that all the city was moved about them,
and they said, *Is this N_____*?
V.20 And she said unto them, Call me not Naomi,
call me Mara: for *the A_____ hath dealt
very b_____ with me.*
V.21 *I went out f_____* and the LORD hath *brought
me home again e_____*: why then call ye me
Naomi, seeing the LORD hath *t_____
a_____* me, and the Almighty hath afflicted
me?

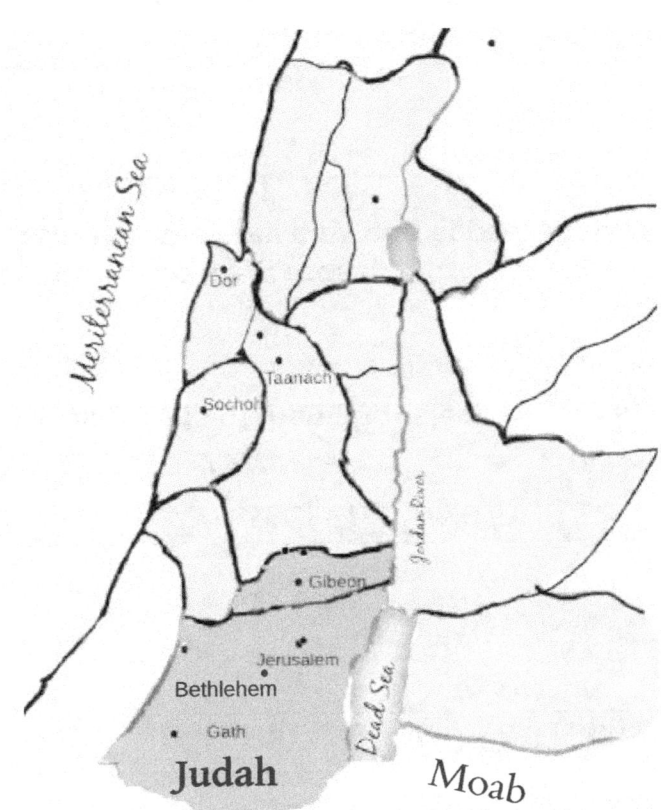

Naomi

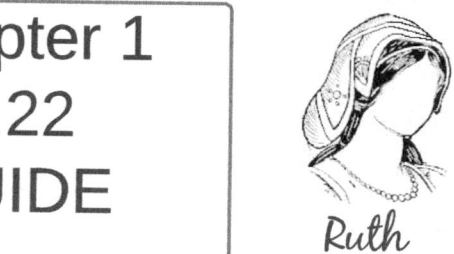

Ruth
Gentile Bride
(Church)

Naomi
Jewish Nation

V.22 So Naomi returned, and Ruth the Moabitess, her daughter in law, with her, which *returned* out of the country of *Moab:* and they came to *Bethlehem* in the *beginning of barley harvest.*

Barley is the first harvest of the season. The beginning of the barley harvest, is observed as the Harvest of The Firstfruits. Bread is made from the barley harvest.

Ruth's arrival at the time of the Harvest of the Firstfruits is symbolic of the arrival of Jesus Christ, the first fruits of the dead and the bread of life.

Naomi led Ruth to Jerusalem during the barley harvest.
They were coming out of a dead godless country.

The Jewish Nation led the Gentile Bride to Bethlehem at the time of the Feast of the Firstfruits. Jesus Christ was the firstfruits from the dead when He arose at the resurrection.

1Corinthians 15:20 But now is **Christ risen from the dead, and become the firstfruits of them that slept.**

(harvest is symbolic of resurrection)

The opened graves were the harvest of the barley season.

Matthew 27:52 And the graves were opened; and many bodies of the saints which slept arose,
Matthew 27:53 And came out of the graves after his resurrection, and went into the holy city, and appeared unto many.

(The first fruits offering of Jesus representing the church after His resurrection.)

Ruth
Gentile Bride
(Church)

Naomi
Jewish Nation

V.22 So Naomi returned, and Ruth the Moabitess, her daughter in law, with her, which *returned* out of the country of M_____: and they came to B_____ in the b_____ of b_____ h_____.

Read Chapter 2

John 6:63...the words that I speak unto you, they are spirit, and they are life.

BOAZ/CHRIST SIMILITUDES

V.1 And Naomi had a kinsman of her husband's, a *mighty man of wealth*, of the *family of Elimelech*; and his name was *Boaz*.

Likeness, similiarity

Similitude

Similitude

Jesus Christ

Genesis 49:10 The <u>sceptre</u> shall not depart <u>from Judah,</u> nor a lawgiver from between his feet, until Shiloh come; and unto him shall the gathering of the people be.

<u>Kinsman</u> Redeemer

The Saviour would come from the Tribe of Judah. Boaz was a near kin of Elimelech who was from Bethlehem in Judah

Jesus Christ

Psalm 24:1 <u>The earth is the LORD's, and the fulness thereof; the world, and they that dwell therein.</u>

Everything belongs to Him, including them that dwell therein

Boaz

1. *Mighty man of Wealth*

2. *Kinsman*

3. *Supplier of Needs*

4. *Lord of the Harvest*

5. *Gives Rest*

6. *Redeemer*

7. *The Bridegroom*

BOAZ/CHRIST SIMILITUDES

Likeness, similiarity

V.1 And Naomi had a kinsman of her husband's, a
m_____ m_____ of w_____, of the
f_____ of E_____; and his
name was B_____.

Boaz

Jesus

1. Mighty man of Wealth

2. Kinsman

3. Supplier of Needs

4. Lord of the Harvest

5. Gives Rest

6. Redeemer

7. The Bridegroom

Naomi (Jewish Nation)

Ruth (Gentile Bride)

Gentile

Ephesians 2:11 Wherefore remember, that ye being in time past Gentiles in the flesh, who are called Uncircumcision by that which is called the Circumcision in the flesh made by hands;
Ephesians 2:12 That at that time ye were without Christ, being aliens from the commonwealth of Israel, and strangers from the covenants of promise, having no hope, and without God in the world:

V.2 And Ruth the *Moabitess* said unto Naomi, *Let me now go* to the field, and glean ears of corn after him in whose sight *I shall find grace.* And she said unto her, Go, my daughter.

Searching for grace.

Ruth confesses that it is nothing she has done to deserve to reap the benefits of the harvest. It is by the grace of the Lord of the Harvest that she allowed to glean in His field.

As a widow and a Gentile in the land, Ruth was hopeless without the grace that would be bestowed upon her. Through this grace she would also provide for Naomi.

Matthew 7:7 Ask, and it shall be given you; seek, and ye shall find; knock, and it shall be opened unto you:

V.3 And *she went*, and came, and *gleaned in the field* after the reapers: and *her hap* was to light on a part of the *field belonging unto Boaz,* who was of the kindred of Elimelech.

The Jewish Nation would be blessed by the grace of God that was bestowed upon the Gentile Bride (Church).

The Old Testament Law of Gleaning

Leviticus 19:9 And when ye reap the harvest of your land, thou shalt not wholly reap the corners of thy field, neither shalt thou gather the gleanings of thy harvest.
Leviticus 19:10 And thou shalt not glean thy vineyard, neither shalt thou gather every grape of thy vineyard; thou shalt leave them for the poor and stranger: I am the LORD your God.

Chapter 2
V.2-3
NOTES

Naomi (Jewish Nation)   Ruth (Gentile Bride)

V.2 And Ruth the M_____ said
unto Naomi, L_____ m_____ n_____
g____ to the field, and glean ears of corn
after him in whose sight ___ s_____
f_____ g_____. And she said unto
her, Go, my daughter.

V.3 And s_____ w_____, and came,
and g_____ in the f_____ after
the reapers: and h_____ h_____ was to
light on a part of the f_____
f_____ u_____
B_____, who was of the kindred of
Elimelech.

Laws of Gleaning GUIDE

Gleaning of the Gentiles

Naomi (Jewish Nation)

Ruth (Gentile) Dog

(Dogs)

Matthew 15:24 But he answered and said, I am not sent but unto the lost sheep of the house of Israel.

Matthew 15:25 Then came she and worshipped him, saying, Lord, help me.

Matthew 15:26 But he answered and said, <u>It is not meet to take the</u> children's bread, <u>and to cast it to</u> dogs.

Matthew 15:27 And she said, Truth, Lord: yet the dogs eat of the crumbs which fall from their masters' table.

Matthew 15:28 Then Jesus answered and said unto her, <u>O woman, great is thy faith: be it unto thee even as thou wilt.</u>

Ruth (the Gentile dog) will glean of the crumbs meant for the children of Israel.

Dogs are symbolic of the Gentiles.

Romans 1:16 For I am not ashamed of the gospel of Christ: for it is the power of God unto <u>salvation to every one that believeth; to the Jew first,</u> and also to the Greek.

The Old Testament Law of Gleaning

Leviticus 19:9 And <u>when ye reap the harvest of your land, thou shalt</u> not wholly reap the corners of thy field, neither <u>shalt thou gather the</u> gleanings <u>of thy harvest.</u>

Leviticus 19:10 And thou shalt not glean thy vineyard, neither shalt thou gather every grape of thy vineyard; <u>thou shalt</u> leave them for the poor and stranger: <u>I am the LORD your God.</u>

<table>
<tr><td>

Laws of
Gleaning
NOTES

</td><td>

Gleaning of the Gentiles

Naomi (Jewish Nation)   *Ruth (Gentile)*

</td></tr>
</table>

Matthew 15:24 But he answered and said, I am not sent but unto the lost sheep of the house of Israel.
Matthew 15:25 Then came she and worshipped him, saying, Lord, help me.
Matthew 15:26 But he answered and said, <u>It is not meet to take the</u> c_____ b_____, <u>and to cast it to</u> d_____.
Matthew 15:27 And she said, Truth, Lord: y_____ the d_____ e_____ of the c_____ which f_____ from t_____ m_____ t_____.
Matthew 15:28 Then Jesus answered and said unto her, <u>O woman, great is thy faith: be it unto thee even as thou wilt.</u>

The Old Testament Law of Gleaning

Leviticus 19:9 And <u>when ye reap the harvest of your land, thou shalt</u> n_____ w_____ r_____ the c_____ of thy f_____, n_____ **shalt thou gather the** g_____ **of thy harvest.**
Leviticus 19:10 And thou shalt not glean thy vineyard, neither shalt thou gather every grape of thy vineyard; <u>thou shalt</u> l_____ them for the p_____ and s_____: <u>I am the LORD your God.</u>

Ruth 2:4 And, behold, *Boaz came from Bethlehem,* and said unto the reapers, The LORD be with you. And they answered him, The LORD bless thee.

Jesus

Servant

Boaz

It is the Holy Spirit that introduces us to Jesus.

Holy Spirit

① *V. 5 Whose damsel is this?*

Ruth decided to come out of the world and was seeking grace from Jesus.

It was also a servant that introduced Isaac to his bride, Gen 24

The Holy Spirit introduces the Gentile Bride (Church) to Jesus.

Ruth

(Jesus) *(Holy Spirit)*

V.5 Then said *Boaz* unto his *servant* that was set over the reapers, *Whose* damsel is this?

V.6 And the *servant* that was set over the reapers answered and said, It is the *Moabitish damsel that* came back with Naomi *out of the country of Moab:* *(out of the world)*

(praying for grace as gentile for the blessings that were meant for Israel).

V.7 And she said, *I pray you, let me glean and gather* after the reapers among the sheaves: so she came, and hath continued even from the morning until now, that she *tarried a little* in the house.

(stedfast and unwavering)

Ruth 2:4 And, behold, B_____ c_____ f_____
B_____, and said unto the reapers, The LORD be
with you. And they answered him, The LORD bless thee.

Servant

Boaz

V. 5 W_____
(1) damsel is this?

Ruth

V.5 Then said B_____ unto his s_____ that was set over the reapers, W_____
damsel is this?

V.6 And the s_____ that was set over the reapers answered and said, It is the
M_____ d_____ that came back with Naomi o_____ of the
country of M_____:

V.7 And she said, I p_____ you, let me g_____ and g_____ after the reapers
among the sheaves: so she came, and hath continued even from the morning until now, that she
t_____ a l_____ in the house.

The conversation between Boaz and Ruth is similiar to that of Jesus and the woman at the well of Samaria, another Gentile woman.

John 4:7 There cometh a woman of Samaria to draw water: Jesus saith unto her, Give me to drink.

Boaz

Ruth

Because he represents Jesus

3

V.10 Then she *fell on her face,* and *bowed herself* to the ground, and said unto him, Why have I found grace in thine eyes, that thou shouldest take knowledge of me, *seeing* I am a stranger?

Not as Elimelech who went looking in other fields.

She went out seeking grace.

Cannot understand God's grace.

Matthew 11:15 He that hath ears to hear, let him hear.

1 V.8 *Hearest thou not,* my daughter? *Go not to glean in another field,* neither go from hence, but abide here fast by my maidens:

2 V.9 Let thine eyes be on the field that they do reap, and go thou after them: have I not charged the *young men* that they *shall not touch thee?* and when thou art athirst, go unto the vessels, and *drink of that which the young men have drawn.*

Not only providing for her but protecting her as His future bride.

Ruth did not have to draw the water herself. It was provided for her.

John 4:14 But whosoever <u>drinketh of the water that I shall give him</u> shall never thirst; but the water that I shall give him shall be in him a well of water springing up into everlasting life.

John 4:15 The woman saith unto him, Sir, give me this water, that I thirst not, <u>neither come hither to draw.</u>

Boaz

Ruth

3

V.10 Then she f_____ on her f_____ and b_____ h_____ to the ground, and said unto him, Why have I found grace in thine eyes, that thou shouldest take knowledge of me, s_____ I am a stranger?

1 V.8 H_____ t_____ n_____, my daughter? G_____ n_____ to g_____ in a_____ f_____, neither go from hence, but abide here fast by my maidens:

2 V.9 Let thine eyes be on the field that they do reap, and go thou after them: have I not charged the y_____ m_____ that they s_____ n_____ t_____ t_____? and when thou art athirst, go unto the vessels, and d_____ of that which the y_____ m_____ h_____ d_____.

Luke 8:17 For nothing is secret, that shall not be made manifest; neither any thing hid, that shall not be known and come abroad.

Boaz

① ②

John 4:29 Come, see a man, which told me all things that ever I did: is not this the Christ?

Showed by the servant (Holy Spirit)

Ruth

forsaken all

V.11 And *Boaz* answered and said unto her, It hath *fully* been *shewed me, all that thou hast done* unto thy mother in law since the death of thine husband: and how thou hast *left thy father and thy mother, and the land of thy nativity*, and art come unto all people which thou knewest not heretofore.

John 4:29 Come, see a man, which told me all things that ever I did: is not this the Christ?

Colossians 3:23-24
Whatever you do, <u>do your work heartily,</u> as for the Lord rather than for men, knowing that from the Lord you <u>will receive the reward of the inheritance.</u> It is the Lord Christ whom you serve.

Jesus Christ Supplier of Needs

V.12 The LORD recompense thy work, and a *full reward* be given thee of the LORD God of Israel, *under whose wings* thou art come to trust.

Similitude

V.13 Then she said, Let me find favour in thy sight, *my lord*; for that *thou hast comforted me*, and for that thou hast spoken friendly unto thine handmaid, though I be not like unto one of thine handmaidens.

Ruth 2:14 And Boaz said unto her, At *mealtime* come thou hither, and *eat of the bread*, and dip thy morsel in the vinegar. And she sat beside the reapers: and *he reached her parched corn*, and she *did eat*, and *was sufficed*, and left.

satisfied

Leviticus 23:14 <u>And ye shall eat neither bread, nor parched corn</u>, nor green ears, <u>until the selfsame day that ye have brought an offering unto your God:</u>

The wave offering at the beginning of the barley harvest had already happened.

Boaz

2

Ruth

1 V.11 And B_____ answered and said unto her, It hath f_____ been s_____ m____, a_____ that t_____ h_____ d_____ unto thy mother in law since the death of thine husband: and how thou hast l_____ thy f_____ and t_____ m_____, and the l_____ of thy n_____, and art come unto all people which thou knewest not heretofore.

V.12 The LORD recompense thy work, and a f_____ r_____ be given thee of the LORD God of Israel, u_____ w_____ w_____ thou art come to trust.

V.13 Then she said, Let me find favour in thy sight, m____ l_____; for that t_____ h_____ c_____ me, and for that thou hast spoken friendly unto thine handmaid, though I be not like unto one of thine handmaidens.

Ruth 2:14 And Boaz said unto her, At m_____ come thou hither, and e_____ of the b_____, and dip thy morsel in the vinegar. And she sat beside the reapers: and h____ reached her p_____ c_____, and she d_____ e_____, and w_____ s_____, and left.

Ruth
Gentile Bride

Naomi

Jewish Nation

V.15 And when she was risen up to glean, Boaz commanded his young men, saying, Let her glean even among the sheaves, and reproach her not:

V.16 And let fall also some of the handfuls of purpose for her, and leave them, that she may glean them, and *rebuke her not.* *Gentile Bride (Church) is encourged to glean in the field.*

V.17 So she gleaned in the field until even, and beat out that she had gleaned: and it was about an ephah of barley.

V.18 And she took it up, and went into the city: and her mother in law saw what she had gleaned: and she brought forth, and *gave to her that she had reserved after she was sufficed.*

Acts 16:31 ... and thou shalt be saved, and thy house.

V.19 And her *mother in law* said unto her, Where hast *thou gleaned* to day? and *where wroughtest* thou? blessed be he that did take knowledge of thee. And she shewed her mother in law with whom she had wrought, and said, The man's name with whom I wrought to day is *Boaz.*

Naomi is the mother of Ruth through the law. (Married to her son.)
The Jewish nation is the mother of the Gentile Bride through the law. (Married to her son, Jesus Christ.)

Ruth
Gentile Bride

Naomi

Jewish Nation

V.15 And when she was risen up to glean, Boaz commanded his young men, saying, Let her glean even among the sheaves, and reproach her not:

V.16 And let fall also some of the handfuls of purpose for her, and leave them, that she may glean them, and r_____ h____ n_____.

V.17 So she gleaned in the field until even, and beat out that she had gleaned: and it was about an ephah of barley.

V.18 And she took it up, and went into the city: and her mother in law saw what she had gleaned: and she brought forth, and g_____ to h____ that she had r_____ a_____ s____ was s_____.

V.19 And her m_____ in l_____ said unto her, Where hast t_____ g_____ to day? and w_____ w_____ thou? blessed be he that did take knowledge of thee. And she shewed her mother in law with whom she had wrought, and said, The man's name with whom I wrought to day is B_____.

Chapter 2 V.20-22 GUIDE

1 V.20 ...*Blessed be he of the LORD*, who hath not left off his *kindness to the living and to the dead.* And Naomi said unto her, The *man is near of kin unto us, one of our next kinsmen.*

Jesus is kind to us while we are living and then resurrects us after we are dead

Naomi tells Ruth that Boaz is near kin to them.

The Jewish nation tells the Gentile Bride (Church) of their relationship to the Saviour. He is near kin to Israel.

Ruth

Gentile Bride (Church)

Naomi

Jewish Nation

2

V. 21 He said unto me also, Thou shalt keep fast by *my young men,* until they have *ended all my harvest.*

provided for her protection.

Similitude

Matthew 9:38 Pray ye therefore the <u>Lord of the harvest,</u> that he will send forth labourers into his harvest.

Jesus Christ Lord of the Harvest

3

V.22 it is good, my daughter, that thou go out *with his maidens,* that they meet thee not in any other field.

1 V.20 ...B_____ be h__ of the L_____, who hath not left off his k_____ to the l_____ and to the d_____. And Naomi said unto her, The m_____ is n_____ of k_____ unto us, one of our n_____ kinsmen.

Ruth

Gentile Bride
(Church)

Naomi

Jewish Nation

2

V. 21 He said unto me also, Thou shalt keep fast by m_____ young men, until they have ended all m____ h_____.

3 V.22 it is good, my daughter, that thou go out with his m_____, that they meet thee not in any other field.

Chapter 2
V.23
GUIDE

Ruth
Gentile Bride
(Church)

Naomi
Jewish Nation

V.23 So she kept fast by the maidens of Boaz to glean unto the *end of barley harvest* and of *wheat harvest*; and dwelt with her mother in law.

Firstfruits

Pentecost

Ruth
Gentile Bride
(Church)

Naomi
Jewish Nation

V.23 So she kept fast by the maidens of Boaz to glean unto the e_____ of b_____ h_____ and of w_____ h_____; and dwelt with her mother in law.

Jewish Feasts GUIDE

The 7 Jewish Feasts Points to the New Testament of Christ

Romans 6:23 For the wages of sin is death; *The wages of sin is death. Death could not hold Jesus because He did not need to pay the wages of sin.*

(Lev. 23:5) 1. Passover — *The Cross*

John 1:29 Behold the *Lamb of God*, which taketh away the sin of the world.

(Lev. 23:6) 2. Unleavened Bread — *Sinless life (death could not hold Him)*

Acts 2:24 Whom God hath raised up,...because it was *not possible* that he should be holden of it.

Barley Harvest (Lev. 23:10) 3. Firstfruits — *Resurrection*

Ruth

1Corinthians 15:20 But now is *Christ risen* from the dead, and become *the firstfruits* of them that slept.

Wheat Harvest (Lev. 23:16) 4. Pentecost — *Holy Spirit Given*

Acts 2:1-4 And when the *day of Pentecost* was fully come...And they were all filled with the *Holy Ghost,*

(Lev. 23:24) 5. Trumpets — *Rapture*

1Corinthians 15:52 In a moment, in the twinkling of an eye, at the last trump: for the *trumpet shall sound,* ....

(Lev. 23:27) 6. Day of Atonement — *Jewish nation brought back into the fold*

Romans 11:26 And so *all Israel shall be saved:* as it is written, ...

(Lev. 23:34) 7. Feast of Tabernacles — *Millenial Reign*

Revelation 20:4and *they lived and reigned with Christ* a thousand years.

The 7 Jewish Feasts Points to the New Testament of Christ

Jewish Feasts NOTES

1. Passover
(Lev. 23:5)

The Cross

John 1:29 Behold the L_____ of G_____, which taketh away the sin of the world.

(Lev. 23:6) **2. Unleavened Bread**

Sinless life (death could not hold Him)

Acts 2:24 Whom God hath raised up,...because it was n_____ p_____ that he should be holden of it.

(Lev. 23:10) **3. Firstfruits**

Resurrection

1Corinthians 15:20 But now is C_____ r_____ from the dead, and become *the* f_____ of them that slept.

(Lev. 23:16) **4. Pentecost**

Holy Spirit Given

Acts 2:1-4 And when the *day of* P_____ was fully come...And they were all filled with the H_____ G_____,

(Lev. 23:24) **5. Trumpets**

Rapture

1Corinthians 15:52 In a moment, in the twinkling of an eye, at the last trump: for the t_____ shall s_____, ...

(Lev. 23:27) **6. Day of Atonement**

Jewish nation brought back into the fold

Romans 11:26 And so a_____ I_____ shall be s_____: as it is written, ...

(Lev. 23:34) **7. Feast of Tabernacles**

Millenial Reign

Revelation 20:4and *they* l_____ *and* r_____ *with* C_____ a thousand years.

Pentecost and the Book of Ruth
GUIDE

V.23 So she kept fast by the maidens of Boaz to glean unto the *end of barley harvest* **and of** *wheat harvest;* **and dwelt with her mother in law.**

Pente means 50.

50 days

Feast of Firstfruits

Ruth 1:22 So Naomi returned, and Ruth ... and they came to Bethlehem in the beginning of barley harvest.

Pentecost—Celebrated at the end of the wheat harvest which is 50 days after the Feast of the Firstfruits.

General Knowledge – Today the Jews read the Book of Ruth on the Day of Pentecost.

Ruth (a gentile) is redeemed by Boaz (Jesus Christ) and became part of the nation of Israel at the end of the wheat harvest (Pentecost).

The Holy Spirit was given to the church at Pentecost and all nations were present.

The Book of Ruth ends with the word David and is a historical genealogy of the Jesus Christ.

Pentecost and the
Book of Ruth
NOTES

V.23 So she kept fast by the maidens of Boaz to glean unto the *end of barley harvest* and of *wheat harvest;* and dwelt with her mother in law.

The Book of Ruth ends with the word David and is a historical genealogy of the Jesus Christ.

Pentecost and the Covenants

Pentecost and the Covenants

Grace

Jeremiah 31:31 Behold, the days come, saith the LORD, that I will <u>make a</u> *new covenant* **with the house of Israel, and with the house of Judah:**

Jeremiah 31:32 *Not according to the covenant* *Law* **<u>that I made with their fathers in the day that I took them by the hand to bring them out of the land of Egypt;</u> which my** *covenant they brake,* **although <u>I was an husband</u> unto them, saith the LORD:**

tablets of stone

Jeremiah 31:33 *But this shall be the covenant* **that I will make with the house of Israel; After those days, saith the LORD, <u>I will put my law in their inward parts, and</u>** *write it in their hearts;* **<u>and will be their God, and they shall be my people.</u>**

Holy Spirit

Old Covenant Law

Left Egypt on Passover was 1st month 15th day to the beginning of the 3rd month is 45 days.

Exodus 19:<u>1</u> *In the third month,* **<u>when the children of Israel were gone forth out of the land of Egypt,</u> the <u>same day</u> came they into the** *wilderness of Sinai.*

The next day, Moses went up Mt. Sinai while the people purified themselves 3 days. This would be the <u>4th</u> day of the 3rd month.

45 days arrived +4 days=49 days. Moses went upon Mt. Sinai and received the law on the next day.

The law was written on tablets of stone. When Israel sinned tablets of stone were broken. The law is written in our hearts, when we sin hearts are broken.

New Covenant Grace

Acts 2:1 And when the *day of Pentecost* **was fully come, they were all with one accord in one place.**

Acts 2:2 And suddenly there came a sound from heaven as of a rushing mighty wind, and it filled all the house where they were sitting.

Acts 2:3 And there appeared unto them cloven tongues like as of fire, and it sat upon each of them.

Acts 2:4 And they were *all filled with the Holy Ghost,* **and began to speak with other tongues, as the Spirit gave them utterance.**

Jesus is both the Passover Lamb and the Firstfruits.

50 days after the Firstfruits, the Holy Spirit (new covenant) was given at Pentecost.

50 days after Passover, the law (old covenant) was given on the same day as Pentecost.

Pentecost and the Covenants

Jeremiah 31:31 Behold, the days come, saith the LORD, that I will <u>make a</u> h_____ c_____ with the house of Israel, and with the house of Judah:

Jeremiah 31:32 N_____ a_____ to the c_____ <u>that I made with their fathers in the day that I took them by the hand to bring them out of the land of Egypt;</u> which my c_____ they b_____, although <u>I was an husband</u> unto them, saith the LORD:

Jeremiah 31:33 B_____ this shall be the c_____ that I will make with the house of Israel; After those days, saith the LORD, <u>I will put my law in their inward parts, and</u> w_____ it in t_____ h_____; <u>and will be their God, and they shall be my people.</u>

Old Covenant Law

Exodus 19:1 In the t_____ m_____, <u>when the children of Israel were gone forth out of the land of Egypt,</u> the <u>same day</u> came they into the w_____ of S_____.

New Covenant Grace

Acts 2:1 And when the d_____ of P_____ was fully come, they were all with one accord in one place.

Acts 2:2 And suddenly there came a sound from heaven as of a rushing mighty wind, and it filled all the house where they were sitting.

Acts 2:3 And there appeared unto them cloven tongues like as of fire, and it sat upon each of them.

Acts 2:4 And they were all f_____ with the H_____ g_____, and began to speak with other tongues, as the Spirit gave them utterance.

Pentecost Similitudes of Old and New Covenants

Similitudes of Old and New Covenants

Old Testament-Sinai (Law)

New Testament-Zion (Grace)

2Corinthians 3:6 for the letter killeth, but the spirit giveth life.

(the letter of the law killeth)

Not one letter will be left out of God's law.

Matthew 5:18 For verily I say unto you, Till heaven and earth pass, one jot or one tittle shall in no wise pass from the law, till all be fulfilled.

Israel is *saved by the blood* of the Passover Lamb. *(Exodus 12:20-21)*

The *Law* was given 50 days after *Passover* See Exodus 19

The *Law* was written on *tablets of stone* by the *finger of God* (Exodus 31:18)

3000 people died as a result of *sin* (Exodus 32:28)

A people newly delivered from Egypt (bondage) *Exodus 15:13*

the LORD came in a *fire* (Exodus 19:18)

the law is a *schoolmaster* (teacher) (Gal.3:24)

The world is *saved by the blood* of the Lamb (Jesus the Firstfruits Resurrection) . *Rev. 12:11*

The Holy Spirit was given on *Pentecost*, 50 days after the Firstfruits (Resurrection) (Acts 2:1)

The *Law* was written *in the hearts by the Holy Spirit* (Hebrews 10:16)

3000 People were added to the church as a result of *repentance* (Acts 2:41)

A people newly delivered from bondage (sin) (Acts 2:38)

the Holy Spirit came with tongues of *fire* (Acts 2:3)

the Holy Spirit *will teach* you of all things (John 14:26)

Pentecost Similitudes of Old and New Covenants

Similitudes of Old and New Covenants

Old Testament-Sinai (Law)

Israel is s_____ by the b_____ of the Passover Lamb. *(Exodus 12:20-21)*

The L_____ was given 50 days after P_____ *See Exodus 19*

The L_____ was written on t_____ of s_____ by the f_____ of g_____ *(Exodus 31:18)*

3_____ people died as a result of s____ *(Exodus 32:28)*

A people newly delivered from Egypt (bondage) *Exodus 15:13*

the LORD came in a f_____ *(Exodus 19:18)*

the law is a s_____ (teacher) *(Gal.3:24)*

New Testament-Zion (Grace)

The world is s_____ by the b_____ of Lamb (Jesus the Firstfruits of theResurrection) . *Rev. 12:11*

The H_____ S_____ was given on P_____, 50 days after the Firstfruits (Resurrection) *(Acts 2:1)*

The L_____ was written in the h_____ by the H_____ S_____ *(Hebrews 10:16)*

3_____ People were added to the church as a result of r_____ *(Acts 2:41)*

A people newly delivered from bondage (sin) *(Acts 2:38)*

the Holy Spirit came with tongues of f_____ *(Acts 2:3)*

the Holy Spirit w_____ t_____ you of all things *(John 14:26)*

Read Chapter 3

Psalm 119:105 Thy word is a lamp unto my feet, and a light unto my path.

Ruth
Gentile Bride
(Church)

Naomi
Jewish Nation

**Matthew 11:28
Come unto me, all ye that labour and are heavy laden, and I will give you rest.**

Jesus Christ

Similitude

Naomi does not take rest in Boaz but instead seeks rest for Ruth.

The Jewish Nation does not take rest in the Messiah but instead points the Gentile Bride (Church) toward this rest.

V.1 Then Naomi her mother in law said unto her, My daughter, shall I not seek rest for thee, that it may be well with thee?

V.2 And now is not Boaz of our kindred, with whose maidens thou wast? Behold, he winnoweth barley to night in the threshingfloor.

Jesus
threshingfloor

Matthew 3:12 Whose fan is in his hand, and he will throughly purge his floor, and gather his wheat into the garner; but he will burn up the chaff with unquenchable fire.

unbelievers in the Lake of fire

The threshingfloor is where the chaff is separated from the grain by winnowing.

The Gentile Bride (Church) will be separated from unbelievers. The unbelievers are considered the chaff and are sifted and burnt.

Revelation 20:11 And I saw a great white throne, and him that sat on it, from whose face the earth and the heaven fled away; and there was found no place for them.

Revelation 20:12 And I saw the dead, small and great, stand before God; and the books were opened: and another book was opened, which is the book of life: and the dead were judged out of those things which were written in the books, according to their works.

Revelation 20:13 And the sea gave up the dead which were in it; and death and hell delivered up the dead which were in them: and they were judged every man according to their works.

Revelation 20:14 And death and hell were cast into the lake of fire. This is the second death.

Ruth
Gentile Bride
(Church)

Naomi
Jewish Nation

V.1 Then Naomi her mother in law said unto her, My d_____, shall I not s_____ r_____ for thee, that it may be well with thee?

V.2 And now is not B_____ of o_____ k_____, with whose maidens thou wast? Behold, he w_____ b_____ to night in the t_____.

First Resurrection
1. Firstfruits 2. Main Harvest
GUIDE

The First Resurrection occurs in 3 separate parts (one for each harvest)

Revelation 20:6 Blessed and holy is he that hath _part_ in the first resurrection:

First Resurrection of each harvest is believers only
1. Firstfruits 2. Actual Harvest

John 5:28 Marvel not at this: for the hour is coming, in the which all that are in the graves shall hear his voice, John 5:29 And shall come forth; they that have done good, unto the resurrection of life; and they that have done evil, unto the resurrection of damnation

Each Harvest has 3 parts
1. Firstfruits, 2. Main Harvest 3. Gleanings

FIRST RESURRECTION (Believers)
1. Firstfruits
2. Main Harvest
(First Resurrection)

SECOND RESURRECTION (Unbelievers)
3. Gleaners
(Second Resurrection)

Barley Harvest

1 Firstfruits
Christ

2. Main Harvest
Old Testament Saints

Wheat Harvest

1. Firstfruits
Dead in Christ

2. Main Harvest
Alive in Christ

Grape Harvest

1. Firstfruits
144,000,
2 Witnesses,
Martyred Saints

2. Main Harvest
Believers of the Tribulation

1Corinthians 15:20 But now is Christ risen from the dead, and become the firstfruits of them that slept.

Matthew 27:52 And the graves were opened; and many bodies of the saints which slept arose,

1Thessalonians 4:16 For the Lord himself shall descend from heaven with a shout, with the voice of the archangel, and with the trump of God: and the dead in Christ shall rise first:

1Thessalonians 4:17 Then we which are alive and remain shall be caught up together with them in the clouds, to meet the Lord in the air: and so shall we ever be with the Lord.

Revelation 11:12 And they heard a great voice from heaven saying unto them, Come up hither. And they ascended up to heaven in a cloud; and their enemies beheld them.

First Resurrection
1. First Fruits 2. Main Harvest

First Resurrection of each harvest is believers only
1. Firstfruits 2. Main Harvest

John 5:28 Marvel not at this: for the hour is coming, in the which all that are in the graves shall hear his voice, **John 5:29** And shall come forth; they that have done good, unto the resurrection of life; and they that have done evil, unto the resurrection of damnation

Each Harvest has 3 parts
1. Firstfruits, 2. Main Harvest
3. Gleanings

FIRST RESURRECTION (Believers)
1. Firstfruits
2. Main Harvest
(First Resurrection)

SECOND RESURRECTION (Unbelievers)
3. Gleaners
(Second Resurrection)

Barley Harvest

1. Firstfruits (1 Cor. 15:20)

C_____

2. Main Harvest (Mt. 27:52)

O___ T_____
S_____

Wheat Harvest

1. Firstfruits (1Thess. 4:16)

D_____ in
C_____

2. Main Harvest (1 Thess 4:17)

A_____ in
C_____

Grape Harvest

1. Firstfruits (Rev. 11:12)

144,____, 2 W_____,
M_____
S_____

2. Main Harvest (Rev. 11:12)

B_____ of the
T_____

1Corinthians 15:20 But now is C_____ risen from the dead, and become the b_____ of them that slept.

Matthew 27:52 A_____ the graves were opened; and many b_____ of the saints which slept a_____,

1Thessalonians 4:16 For the Lord himself shall descend from heaven with a shout, with the voice of the archangel, and with the trump of God: and the dead in C_____ shall r_____ f_____:

1Thessalonians 4:17 T_____ we which are a_____ and remain shall be caught up together with them in the c_____, to meet the Lord in the air: and so shall we ever be with the Lord.

Revelation 11:12 And they heard a great voice from heaven saying unto them, C_____ u____ h_____. And they ascended up to heaven in a c_____; and their enemies beheld them.

Second Resurrection
3. Gleaners
GUIDE

Barley Harvest

3.Gleanings
Old Testament
Unbelievers

Wheat Harvest

3. Gleanings
New Testament
Unbelievers

Grape Harvest

3.Gleanings
Tribulation
Unbelievers

The Second Resurrection of each harvest is for unbelievers (3. gleaners). No unbeliever will be resurrected until the Great White Throne Judgment.

Does not represent believers.

Leviticus 19:10 And thou shalt not glean thy vineyard, neither shalt thou gather every grape of thy vineyard; thou shalt leave them for the poor and stranger: I am the LORD your God.

Revelation 20:11 And I saw a great white throne, and him that sat on it, from whose face the earth and the heaven fled away; and there was found no place for them.

Revelation 20:12 And I saw the dead, small and great, stand before God; and the books were opened: and another book was opened, which is the book of life: and the dead were judged out of those things which were written in the books, according to their works.

Revelation 20:13 And the sea gave up the dead which were in it; and death and hell delivered up the dead which were in them: and they were judged every man according to their works.

Revelation 20:14 And death and hell were cast into the lake of fire. This is the second death.

Ephesians 2:8 For by grace are ye saved through faith; and that not of yourselves: it is the gift of God:
Ephesians 2:9 Not of works, lest any man should boast.

Unbelievers had not been resurrected to eternal life

All believers have already been resurrected

Unbelievers are judged according to their works at the Great White Throne Judgment. Their works cannot pay for their sins and they will fall short of salvation.

Believers will not be at the Great White Throne judgment because they will not be judged according to their works. Righteousness has been imputed to them through faith not works.

Second Resurrection
3. Gleaners
NOTES

Barley Harvest

3.Gleanings

Old Testament

U_____

Wheat Harvest

3. Gleanings

New Testament

U_____

Grape Harvest

3.Gleanings

Tribulation

U_____

The Second Resurrection of each harvest is for unbelievers (3. gleaners). No unbeliever will be resurrected until the Great White Throne Judgment.

Leviticus 19:10 And thou shalt not glean thy vineyard, neither shalt thou gather every grape of thy vineyard; thou shalt leave them for the

p_____ and s_____: I am the LORD your God.

Revelation 20:11 And I saw a g_____
w_____ t_____, and him that sat on it, from whose face the earth and the heaven fled away; and there was found no place for them.

Revelation 20:12 And I saw the d_____, small and great, stand before God; and the books were opened: and another book was opened, which is the book of life: and the d_____ were judged out of those things which were written in the books, according to their works.

Revelation 20:13 And the sea gave up the d_____ which were in it; and death and hell delivered up the d_____ which were in them: and they were judged every man according to their works.

Revelation 20:14 And death and hell were cast into the lake of fire. This is the s_____ d_____.

Naomi told Ruth what she must do to approach Boaz.

The law was given to the Jewish nation who in turn would instruct the Gentile Bride (Church).

Ruth
Gentile Bride
(Church)

Naomi
Jewish Nation

Preparing herself as the Gentile Bride

V.3 *Wash* thyself therefore, and *anoint thee*, and *put thy raiment upon thee*, and get thee down to the floor: but make not thyself known unto the man, until he shall have *done eating and drinking*.

Revelation 19:7 Let us be glad and rejoice, and give honour to him: <u>for the marriage of the Lamb is come, and his wife hath made herself ready.</u>

Wash

Ephesians 5:26 That he might sanctify and <u>cleanse it with the washing of water by the word,</u>
Ephesians 5:27 That he might <u>present it to himself a glorious church,</u> not having spot, or wrinkle, or any such thing; but that it should be holy and without blemish.

Anoint-symbolic of Holy Spirit

Matthew 25:1 Then shall the kingdom of heaven be likened unto ten virgins, which took their lamps, and <u>went forth to meet the bridegroom.</u>
Matthew 25:2 And five of them were wise, and five were foolish.
Matthew 25:3 They that were foolish took their lamps, and took no oil with them:
Matthew 25:4 But <u>the wise took oil in their vessels</u> with their lamps.

raiment

Revelation 21:2 And I John saw the holy city, new Jerusalem, coming down from God out of heaven, *prepared as a bride adorned for her husband.*

He would not eat again until the matter was finished.

Luke 22:16 For I say unto you, <u>I will not any more eat thereof, until it be fulfilled in the kingdom of God.</u>
Luke 22:18 For I say unto you, <u>I will not drink of the fruit of the vine, until the kingdom of God shall come.</u>

Ruth
Gentile Bride
(Church)

Naomi
Jewish Nation

Preparing herself as the Gentile Bride

V.3 *Wash* thyself therefore, and a_____ t_____, and p_____ t_____ r_____
u_____ t_____, and get thee down to the floor: but make not thyself known unto the man,
until he shall have d_____ e_____ *and* d_____.

Ruth
Gentile Bride
(Church)

Naomi
Jewish Nation

V.4 And it shall be, when he lieth down, that thou shalt mark the place where he shall lie, and thou shalt go in, and *uncover his feet*, and *lay thee down; and he will tell thee what thou shalt do.*
V.5 And she said unto her, *All* that thou sayest unto me *I will do.*

The children of Israel when they received the law in the wilderness.

Exodus 24:3 And Moses came and told <u>the people</u> all the words of the LORD, and all the judgments: and all the people answered with one voice, and said, All the words which the LORD hath said will we do.

V.6 And she went down unto the floor, and *did according to all* that her mother in law bade her.
V.7 And *when Boaz had eaten and drunk*, and his heart was merry, he went to lie down at the end of the heap of corn: and *she came softly*, and *uncovered his feet, and laid her down.*

Ruth uncovered his feet as an act of submission. She did not uncover his nakedness. When Boaz awoke to cover his feet, she would tell him not just cover his feet but also to cover her.

Ruth
Gentile Bride
(Church)

Naomi
Jewish Nation

V.4 And it shall be, when he lieth down, that thou shalt mark the place where he shall lie, and thou shalt go in, and u_____ h____ f_____, and l_____ t_____ d_____; and h__ w_____ t_____ t_____ w_____ t_____ s_____ d____.

V.5 And she said unto her, A_____ that thou sayest unto me __ w_____ d__.

V.6 And she went down unto the floor, and d_____ a_____ t__ a____ that her mother in law bade her.

V.7 And w_____ B_____ h____ e_____ and d_____, and his heart was merry, he went to lie down at the end of the heap of corn: and s____ c_____ s_____, and u_____ h____ f_____, and l_____ h_____ d_____.

Chapter 3 V.8-9 GUIDE

The Parable of the 10 Virgins. Midnight was a surprise. It must have seemed like forever that she waited for him to awaken.

Matthew 25:6 And at midnight there was a cry made, Behold, the bridegroom cometh; go ye out to meet him.

Ruth Gentile Bride (Church)

Boaz Jesus Christ

V.8 And it came to pass at midnight, that the man was afraid, and turned himself: and, behold, a woman lay at his feet.

V.9 And he said, Who art thou? And she answered, I am Ruth thine handmaid: spread therefore thy skirt over thine handmaid; for thou art a near kinsman.

The first time they met, Boaz said unto her.
Ruth 2:12 The LORD recompense thy work, and a full reward be given thee of the LORD God of Israel, under whose wings thou art come to trust.

Ruth is asking Boaz, as her near kinsman, to become her redeemer When he covered his feet, she was aking him to spread his wings over her, as well.

The Gentile Bride (Church) is asking for redemption from her redeemer (Jesus).

Ruth
Gentile Bride
(Church)

Boaz
Jesus Christ

V.8 And it came to pass a_____ m_____, that the man was afraid, and turned himself: and, behold, a woman lay at his feet.

V.9 And he said, *Who art thou?* And she answered, I am R_____ t_____ h_____:
s_____ t_____ thy s_____ over t_____ h_____; for t_____ a_____ a n_____ k_____.

Ruth
Gentile Bride
(Church)

Boaz
Jesus Christ

V.10 And he said, Blessed be thou of the LORD, my daughter: for thou hast shewed *more kindness in the latter end than at the beginning, inasmuch as thou followed not young men, whether poor or rich.*

Ruth
Gentile Bride
(Church)

Boaz
Jesus Christ

V.10 And he said, Blessed be thou of the LORD, my daughter: for thou hast shewed m_____ k_____ in the l_____ e_____ than at the b_____, inasmuch as thou f_____ n_____ y_____ m_____, w_____ p_____ or r_____.

Ruth
Gentile Bride (Church)

kinsman nearer than grace – represents the law. Old Testament

Boaz (Jesus) represents grace (New Testament) (law)

V.11 And now, my daughter, fear not; I will do to thee all that thou requirest: for all the city of my people doth know that thou art a virtuous woman. ← Jews

← The Jews will accept the Gentiles

Romans 3:29 Is he the God of the Jews only? is he not also of the Gentiles? Yes, of the Gentiles also:

Grace ⟶ Law ⟶

V.12 And now it is true that I am thy near kinsman: howbeit there is a kinsman nearer than I.

V.13 Tarry this night, and it shall be in the morning, that if he will perform unto thee the part of a kinsman, well; let him do the kinsman's part: but if he will not do the part of a kinsman to thee, then will I do the part of a kinsman to thee, as the LORD liveth: lie down until the morning.

The Boaz agrees to redeem Ruth.
The Jesus agrees to redeem the Gentile Bride (Church).

V.14 And she lay at his feet until the morning: and she rose up before one could know another. And he said, Let it not be known that a woman came into the floor.

V.15 Also he said, Bring the vail that thou hast upon thee, and hold it. And when she held it, he measured six measures of barley, and laid it on her: and she went into the city.

6 measures–1 measure/day. 7th day is rest. He will finish his work before the day of rest.

Ruth
Gentile Bride
(Church)

kinsman nearer
than grace –
represents the
law. Old
Testament

Boaz
(Jesus)
represents   (law)
grace
(New
Testament)

V.11 And now, my daughter, f_____ n_____; __ w_____ d_____ to t_____ a_____ that thou r_____: for a____ the c_____ of my p_____ doth know that thou art a v_____ woman.

V.12 And now it is true that I am thy n_____ k_____: howbeit there is a k_____ n_____ than _____.

V.13 Tarry this night, and it shall be in the morning, that if he will perform unto thee the part of a kinsman, well; let him do the kinsman's part: but if he w_____ n_____ do the part of a k_____ to thee, then w_____ I do the p_____ of a k_____ to thee, as the LORD liveth: lie down until the morning.

V.14 And she lay at his feet until the morning: and s_____ rose up b_____ one c_____ k_____ a_____. And he said, Let it not be known that a woman came into the floor.

V.15 Also he said, B_____ the v_____ that thou h_____ u_____ t_____, and hold it. And when she held it, he measured s_____ m_____ of b_____, and laid it on her: and she went into the c_____.

...the part of a kinsman... Ruth 3:13

Boaz

Buy back, ransom or bring back from captivity.

1. Redeem property his brother sold as a result of poverty

Leviticus 25:25 If thy brother be *waxen poor*, and hath sold away some of his possession, and if any of *his kin* come to *redeem it*, then shall he redeem that which *his brother sold.*

2. Marry the widow of a deceased brother to continue his name

Deuteronomy 25:5 If brethren dwell together, and one of them die, and have no child, the wife of the dead shall not marry without unto a stranger: her *husband's brother shall go in unto her*, and *take her to him to wife*, and perform the duty of an husband's brother unto her.
Deuteronomy 25:6 And it shall be, that *the firstborn* which she beareth shall succeed in the *name of his brother* which is dead, *that his name be not put out of Israel.*

3. The Redeemer from Slavery

4. The Protector and Avenger of Blood

Boaz

Chapter 3 Kinsman-Redeemer NOTES

...the part of a kinsman... Ruth 3:13

→Buy back, ransom or bring back from captivity.

1. Redeem property his brother sold as a result of poverty

Leviticus 25:25 If thy brother be w_____ p_____, and hath sold away some of his possession, and if any of h_____ k_____ come to r_____ it, then shall he redeem that which h_____ b_____ s_____.

2. Marry the widow of a deceased brother to continue his name

Deuteronomy 25:5 If brethren dwell together, and one of them die, and have no child, the wife of the dead shall not marry without unto a stranger: her h_____ b_____ s_____ go in u_____ h_____, and t_____ h_____ to h_____ to w_____, and perform the duty of an husband's brother unto her.
Deuteronomy 25:6 And it shall be, that the f_____ which she beareth shall succeed in the n_____ of h_____ b_____ which is dead, t_____ his n_____ be n_____ p_____ out of I_____.

Ruth
Gentile Bride
(Church)
Naomi
Jewish Nation

Are you the redeemed?

V.16 And when she came to her mother in law, she said, *Who art thou, my daughter?* And she told her all that the man had done to her.

V.17 And she said, These *six measures of barley* gave he me; for he said to me, *Go not empty unto thy mother in law.*

V.18 Then said she, *Sit still*, my daughter, until thou *know how the matter will fall*: for the man *will not be in rest*, until he *have finished the thing* this day.

The six measures of barley is one measure per day representing the days work is done. He will not rest. (Sabbath Day).

Naomi is blessed from Ruth's relationship with Boaz.

The Jewish nation is blessed from the Gentile Bride (Church's) relationship with the Messiah.

Ruth
Gentile Bride
(Church)

Naomi
Jewish Nation

V.16 And when she came to her mother in law, she said, W_____ art t_____, my daughter? And she told her all that the man had done to her.

V.17 And she said, These s_____ m_____ of b_____ gave he me; for he said to me, Go not e_____ unto thy m_____ in l_____.

V.18 Then said she, S_____ s_____, my daughter, until thou k_____ how the m_____ will f_____: for the man w_____ n_____ be in r_____, until he h_____ f_____ the t_____ this day.

Read Chapter 4

Matthew 4:4 But he answered and said, It is written, Man shall not live by bread alone, but by every word that proceedeth out of the mouth of God.

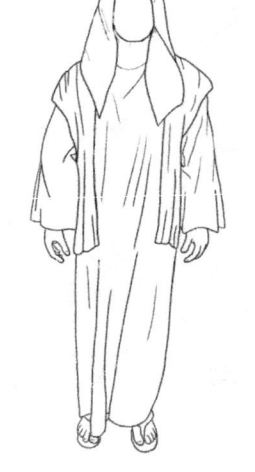

Chapter 4
V.1-2
GUIDE

represents the grace

1 V.1 Then went *Boaz* up to the gate, and *sat* him down there:

2

V.1 And he turned aside, and *sat down.*

V. 1...the *kinsman* of whom Boaz spake *came by*

represents the law

3 V.1 *Ho*, such a one! turn aside, *sit down* here.

4

V.2 And he took *ten* men of the *elders of the city,* and said, Sit ye down here. And they sat down.

represents the 10 commandments (witnesses)

(1) V.1 Then went B_____ up to the g_____, and s_____ him down there:

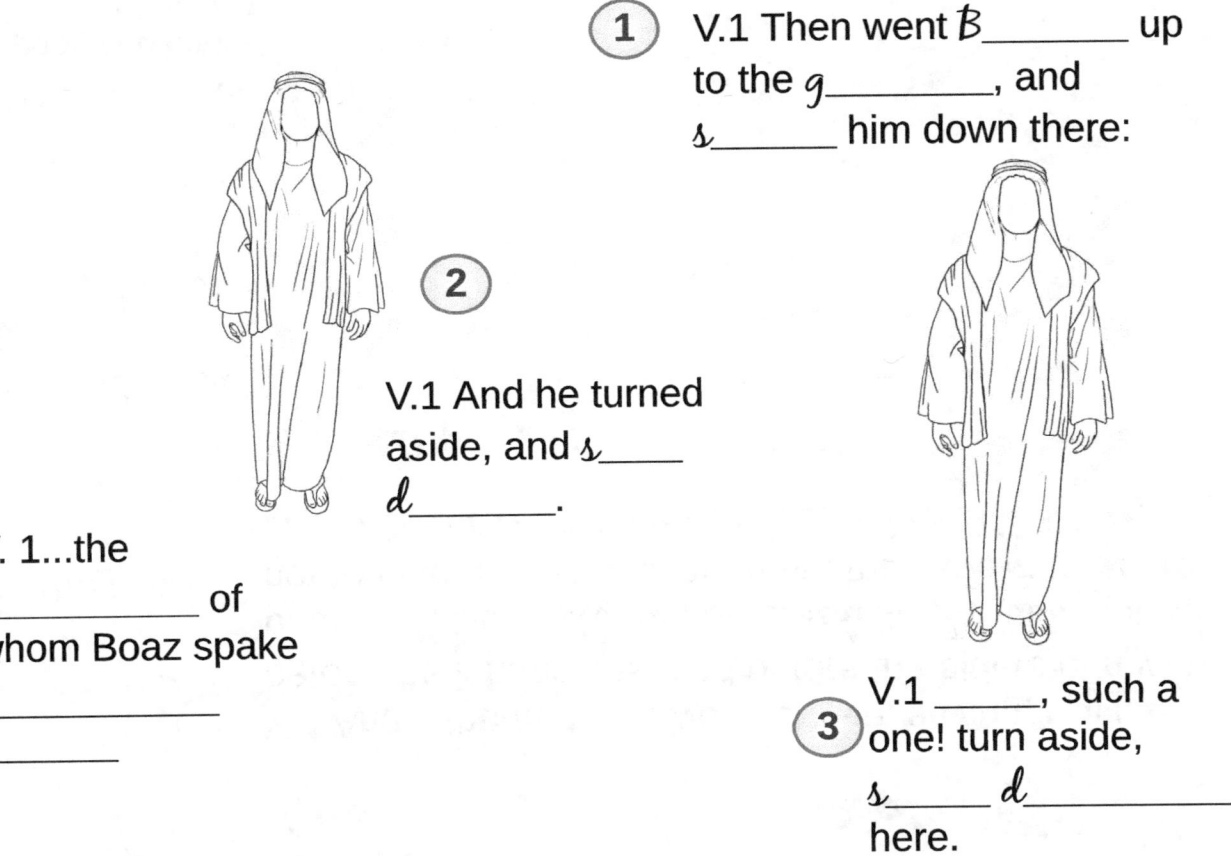

(2) V.1 And he turned aside, and s____ d_____.

V. 1...the k_____ of whom Boaz spake c_____ b_____

(3) V.1 _____, such a one! turn aside, s_____ d_____ here.

(4) V.2 And he took t_____ men of the e_____ of the c_____, and said, Sit ye down here. And they sat down.

Chapter 4 V.3-4 GUIDE

Boaz
Jesus Christ
(Grace)

1 V.3 And he said unto the *kinsman, Naomi,* that is *(The Law)* *(Jewish Nation)* come again out of the country of *Moab,* *(Gentiles)* *selleth a parcel of land,* which was *our brother Elimelech's:*

kinsman
(The Law)

2 V.4 And *I* thought to advertise thee, saying, *Buy* it *(Grace)* *(Purchase)* before the inhabitants, and before the elders of my people. *If thou wilt redeem it, redeem it:* but if thou wilt not redeem it, then tell me, that I may know: for there *is none to redeem it beside thee; and I am after thee.* *(The Law)* *(Grace)*

3 V.4 And he said, *I will redeem it.* *(The Law)*

The law has the ability to redeem the land of Elimelech

Leviticus 25:25 If thy brother be waxen poor, and hath sold away some of his possession, and if any of his kin come to redeem it, then shall he redeem that which his brother sold.

Boaz
Jesus Christ
(Grace)

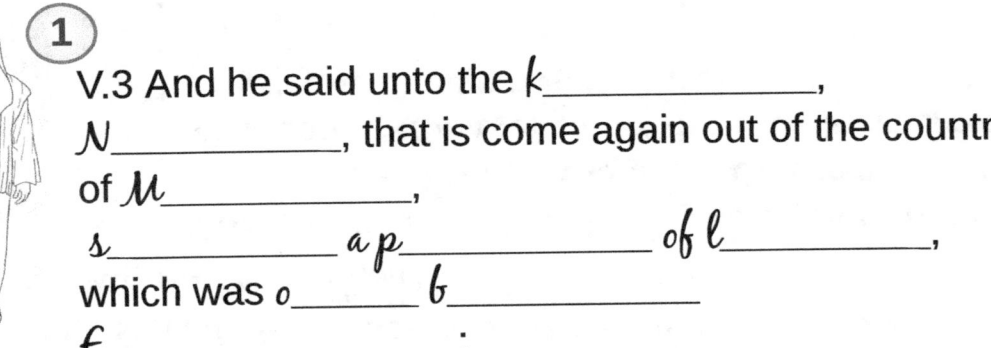

1 V.3 And he said unto the k_____,
N_____, that is come again out of the country
of M_____,
s_____ a p_____ of l_____,
which was o_____ b_____
E_____:

kinsman
(The Law)

2 V.4 And _____ thought to advertise thee, saying,
B_____ it before the inhabitants, and before the
elders of my people. I_____ t_____
w_____ r_____ i__, r_____
i___: but if thou wilt not redeem it, then tell me,
that I may know: for there is n_____ to
r_____ it b_____ thee; and ___ a___
a_____ t_____.

3 V.4 And he said, ___
will r_____
i____.

10 elders of the
city

Boaz
Jesus Christ
(Grace)

1

Jewish nation

ELIMELECH
FATHER

MAHLON
ELDEST SON

(Grace)

(Israel)

V.5 Then *said Boaz,* What day thou *buyest the field* of the *hand of Naomi,* thou must buy it also of *Ruth the Moabitess,* the wife of the dead, *to raise up the name of the dead* upon his *inheritance.*

resurrect the dead
church

Gentile Bride
(Church)

The law says wages of sin is death. It would violate it ownself if it rose up the name of the dead to an inheritance.

(The Law)
near kinsman

2

V.6 And the *kinsman said, I cannot redeem it* for myself, lest I *mar mine own inheritance:* redeem thou *my right to thyself; for I cannot redeem it.*

Romans 8:3 <u>For what the law could not do, in that it was weak through the flesh,</u> God sending his own Son in the likeness of sinful flesh, and for sin, condemned sin in the flesh:

The law is the wages of sin is death.
It cannot resurrect the dead. By God' grace, the sinless blood of Jesus can redeem the church from the law of death.

Chapter 4
V.5-6
NOTES

Boaz

Jesus Christ
(Grace)

①

V.5 Then *said* B_____, What day thou *b*_____ the
*f*_____ of the *h*_____ of *N*_____, thou
must buy it also of *R*_____ the *M*_____, the wife
of the dead, *to r*_____ up the *n*_____ of the
*d*_____ upon his *i*_____.

ELIMELECH FATHER

MAHLON ELDEST SON

10 elders of the city

(The Law)
near kinsman

②

V.6 And the *k*_____ said, I *c*_____
*r*_____ *i*_____ for myself, lest *I*
*m*_____ *m*_____ *o*_____
*i*_____ : *r*_____ *t*_____ my
*r*_____ to *t*_____ ; for ____ *c*_____
*r*_____ *i*____.

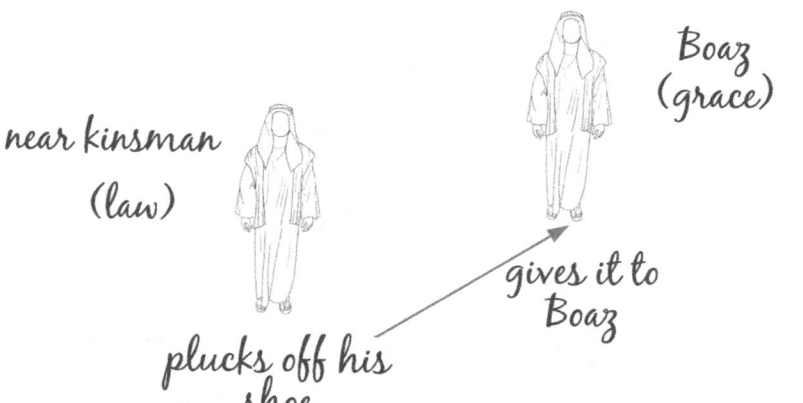

near kinsman
(law)

Boaz
(grace)

gives it to
Boaz

plucks off his
shoe

The near kinsman was not worthy to unloose the latchet of the shoe of Boaz. He must pluck off his own shoe.

10 elders of the city (witnesses)

V.7 Now this was the manner in former time in Israel concerning redeeming and concerning changing, for to confirm all things; a man plucked off his shoe, and gave it to his neighbour: and this was a testimony in Israel.

V.8 Therefore the kinsman said unto Boaz, Buy it for thee. So he drew off his shoe. (law) (grace)

The mother of Jesus and the mother of John were cousins. (kin)

Luke 1:36 And, behold, thy cousin Elisabeth, she hath also conceived a son in her old age: and this is the sixth month with her, who was called barren.

father was a levite priest. (Law)

John the Baptist was a near kinsman to Jesus.

(law)

plucks off his shoe

Jesus
(grace)

gives it to Jesus

Acts 20:28 Take heed therefore unto yourselves, and to all the flock, over the which the Holy Ghost hath made you overseers, to feed the church of God, which he hath purchased with his own blood.

When the priest and Levites asked John the Baptist, if he was the Christ (Redeemer), as a John said, I am not worthy to unloose the latchet of His shoes. It is John that should pluck off his own shoe as a testimony to Jesus, the Redeemer

John 1:27 He it is, who coming after me is preferred before me, whose shoe's latchet I am not worthy to unloose.

near kinsman
(law)

Boaz
(grace)

gives it to
Boaz

plucks off his
shoe

10 elders of the
city (witnesses)

V.7 Now this was the manner in former time in Israel concerning
r_____ and concerning c_____, for to confirm all
things; a man p_____ o_____ his s_____, and gave it to
his neighbour: and this was a t_____ in I_____.
V.8 Therefore the k_____ said unto B_____,
B_____ i___ for t_____. So he drew off h_____
s_____.

(law)

Jesus
(grace)

gives it to
Jesus

plucks off
his shoe

Chapter 4 V.9-10 GUIDE

Boaz
Jesus Christ
Redeemer

1Corinthians 6:20 <u>For ye are bought with a price</u>: therefore glorify God in your body, and in your spirit, which are God's.

①

V.9 *Ye are witnesses* this day, that I have *bought* all that was *Elimelech's*, and all that was *Chilion's and Mahlon's*, of the hand of *Naomi*.

Jews and Gentiles alike

②

V.10 Moreover *Ruth the Moabitess, the wife of Mahlon, have I purchased to be my wife, to raise up the name of the dead upon his inheritance*, that the name of the dead be not cut off from *among his brethren*, and from the gate of his place: ye are *witnesses* this day.

10 elders of the city

witnesses

Boaz
Jesus Christ
Redeemer

1

V.9 Ye are w_____ this day, that I have
b_____ a_____ that was E_____, and
a____ that was C_____ and M_____, of the
hand of N_____.

10 elders of the city

witnesses

2 V.10 Moreover Ruth the M_____, the
wife of M_____, have I
p_____ to be m____ w_____, to
r_____ u____ the n_____ of the
d_____ upon his i_____,
that the name of the dead be not cut off from
a_____ his b_____,
and from the gate of his place: ye are
w_____ this day.

Boaz
Jesus Christ
The Redeemer

V.11 And all the people that were in the gate, and the elders, said, We are witnesses. The LORD make the woman that is come into thine house like Rachel and like Leah, which two did build the house of Israel: and do thou worthily in Ephratah, and be famous in Bethlehem:

Abraham

Isaac

Jacob (also named Israel) ←

1. Reuben
2. Simeon
3. Levi
4. Judah
5. Dan
6. Naphtali
7. Gad
8. Asher
9. Issachar
10. Zebulun
11. Joseph
12 Benjamin

Rachael and Leah were the wives of Jacob (Israel) and brought forth the 12 tribes of Israel, including the tribe of Judah, from whom the coming Messiah would descend.

The woman that is come into thine house of Israel is the Gentile Bride (church), The Lord make the church to build her family like Rachel and Leah built Israel.

From Isaac would the seed of the promised Messiah come. Esau would have been born first but Jacob broke forth in the womb and was born first.

From Judah would the seed of the promised Messiah come. Zarah would have been born first but Pharez broke forth in the womb and was born first.

Boaz
Jesus Christ
The Redeemer

Abraham
Isaac
Jacob (also named Israel)

    1. Reuben
    2. Simeon
    3. Levi
    4. Judah
    5. Dan
    6. Naphtali
    7. Gad
    8. Asher
    9. Issachar
    10. Zebulun
    11. Joseph
    12 Benjamin

V.11 And a_____ t_____ p_____ that were in the gate, and the e_____, said, We are witnesses. The L_____ make the w_____ that is c_____ into t_____ house l_____ R_____ and l_____ L_____, which t_____ did b_____ the h_____ of I_____: and do thou worthily in Ephratah, and be f_____ in B_____:

Boaz
Jesus Christ
Redeemer

Ruth
Gentile Bride
Redeemed

V.12 And let thy house be like the house of Pharez, whom Tamar bare unto Judah, of the seed **which the** LORD shall give **thee of this young woman.**

Genesis 38:26 And Judah acknowledged them, and said, She hath been more righteous than I; because that I gave her not to Shelah my son. And he knew her again no more.

Genesis 38:27 And it came to pass in the time of her travail, that, behold, twins were in her womb. Same as Jacob & Esau

Genesis 38:28 And it came to pass, when she travailed, that the one put out his hand: and the midwife took and bound upon his hand a scarlet thread, saying, This came out first.

Genesis 38:29 And it came to pass, as he drew back his hand, that, behold, his brother came out: and she said, How hast thou broken forth? this breach be upon thee: therefore his name was called Pharez.

Genesis 38:30 And afterward came out his brother, that had the scarlet thread upon his hand: and his name was called Zarah.

Tamar's husband died and she was left a widow. According to Jewish law, her husband's brother was supposed to marry her and raise up children in her husband's name. Judah, her father in law, promised her if she waited for Shelah, her husband's brother to become old enough, that he would give her Shelah for a husband. Judah broke his promise. So Tamar deceived Judah and played a harlot. Through this act of whoredom Pharez was conceived.

Therefore, Pharez was born a bastard and could not enter into the congregation of the Lord for 10 generations by Jewish law. Deut. 23:2 He had a twin brother Zarah, whom should have been born first. They tied a scarlet thread upon Zarah's hand so they knew which should come out first. But Pharez broke forth first. Same as Jacob and Esau. Jacob was blessed because he also broke forth ahead of Esau.

See Chapter 4:18-22.

Boaz
Jesus Christ
Redeemer

Ruth
Gentile Bride
Redeemed

V.12 And let thy house be like the h_____ of P_____, whom
J_____ b_____ unto J_____, of the s_____ which the
L_____ shall g_____ thee of this young woman.

Chapter 4 V.13-15 GUIDE

Boaz
Jesus Christ
Redeemer

Ruth
Gentile Bride
Redeemed

10 elders of the city

(1) V.13 *So Boaz took Ruth, and she was his wife:* and when he went in unto her, the LORD gave her conception, and *she bare a son.*

the women

now has a redeemer

Naomi (Jewish Nation)

(2) V.14 And the *women said* unto Naomi, Blessed be the LORD, which hath *not left thee this day without a kinsman, that his name may be famous in Israel.*

2 Corinthians 5:17 Therefore if any man be in Christ, he is a new creature: old things are passed away; behold, all things are become new.

Grandfather of King David lineage of Jesus Christ.

(3) V.15 And *he shall be unto thee a restorer of thy life,* and a *nourisher of thine old age:* for thy *daughter in law,* which loveth thee, which is better to thee than *seven sons, hath born him.*

(Gentile Bride)

There were 7 generations between Pharez and Obed (Ruth's son). Obed would be better to her than any of these 7 sons.

Boaz
Jesus Christ
Redeemer

Ruth
Gentile Bride
Redeemed

10 elders of the city

the women

Naomi (Jewish Nation)

① V.13 So B_____ took R_____, and s_____ was his w_____: and when he went in unto her, the LORD gave her conception, and s____ b____ ___ _____.

② V.14 And the w_____ said unto Naomi, Blessed be the LORD, which hath n____ l_____ t_____ this d_____ without a k_____, that his n_____ may be f_____ in I_____.

③ V.15 And he shall be unto thee a r_____ of t____ l_____, and a n_____ of thine o_____ age: for thy daughter in law, which loveth thee, which is better to thee than s_____ s_____, hath born him.

Naomi

Naomi was the grandmother to Obed and loved him.

Through the redeemer Boaz, Naomi had a grandson to keep the name of her dead husband, Elimelech alive.

1 V.16 And Naomi took the child, and laid it in her bosom, and became nurse unto it.

The nation of Israel has taken the Gentiles into its bosom and nourished her with the commandments and covenants of the Word.

2 V.17 And the women her neighbours gave it a name, saying, There is a son born to Naomi; and they called his name Obed: he is the father of Jesse, the father of David.

Naomi

1

V.16 And N_____ took the c_____,
and laid it in her bosom, and b_____
n_____ unto it.

2 V.17 And the w_____ h____
n_____ g_____ it a n_____,
saying, There is a s_____ born to N_____;
and they called his name O_____: he is the
f_____ of J_____, the f_____
of D_____.

V.18 Now these are the generations of Pharez: Pharez begat Hezron,

V.19 And Hezron begat Ram, and Ram begat Amminadab,

V.20 And Amminadab begat Nahshon, and Nahshon begat Salmon,

V.21 And Salmon begat Boaz, and Boaz begat Obed,

V.22 And Obed begat Jesse, and Jesse begat David.

Pharez
1

Hezron
2

Ram
3

Amminadab
4

Nahshon
5

Salmon
6

The mother of Boaz was Rahab the harlot. His wife was Ruth, a Moabitess.

Through the grace of God, both of these women are in the genealogy of the Lord Jesus Christ.

Boaz
7

Ruth became the great grandmother of King David.

Obed
8

Jesse
9

David
10

Deuteronomy 23:2
A bastard shall not enter into the congregation of the LORD; even to his tenth generation **shall he not enter into the congregation of the LORD.**

V.18 Now these are the generations of Pharez: **Pharez** begat **Hezron,**
V.19 And Hezron begat **Ram**, and Ram begat **Amminadab,**
V.20 And Amminadab begat Nahshon, and Nahshon begat Salmon,
V.21 And Salmon begat **Boaz**, and Boaz begat **Obed,**

V.22 And Obed begat **Jesse**, and Jesse begat **David.**

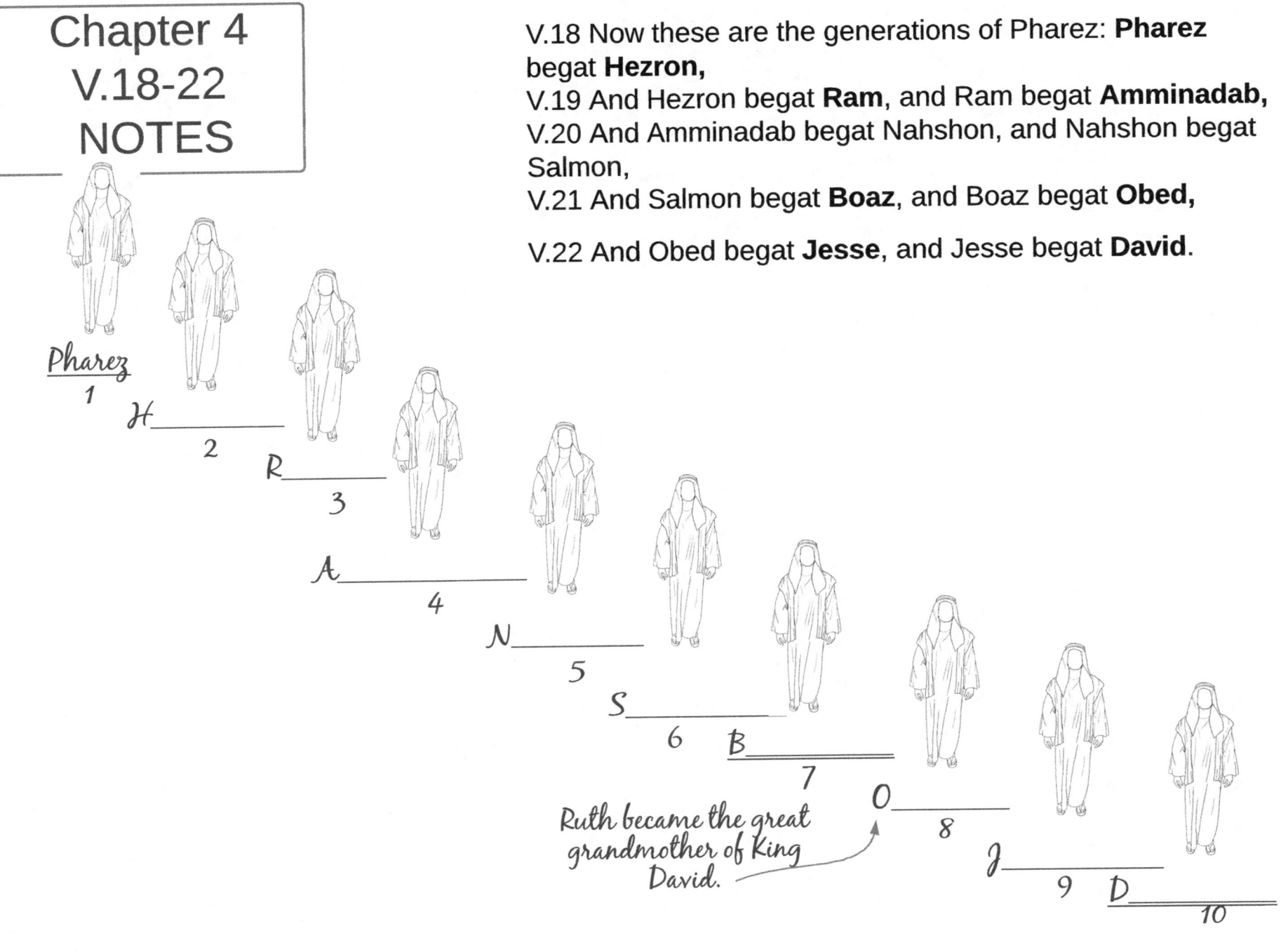

Pharez
1

H_____
2

R_____
3

A_____
4

N_____
5

S_____
6

B_____
7

O_____
8

J_____
9

D_____
10

Ruth became the great grandmother of King David.

To order additional
Common People Series
Bible Study Guides
visit us at
www.CommonPeopleSeries.com

Please join our email list for free lessons and videos. We'll let you know when new Bible Study Guides are being published.

Contact us at
commonpeopleseries@gmail.com